Eyes Wide Open

How an ancient mystery hidden in
both the cosmos and the Bible could bring
about a spiritual awakening in your life

*"To you it has been given to know the secrets of the
kingdom of God"—Luke 8:10*

Martin Trench

Author website: www.martintrench.com

ISBN: 978-1-723910-12-8

Table of Contents

Foreword

Martin Trench is a thinker…and a stirrer; I like that.

In his speaking and writing he forces the listener or reader to stop and think… evaluate past paradigms and look at things from a different viewpoint. This in and of itself is helpful, as our thoughts and beliefs, to be strengthened, must be challenged. Martin also is a stirrer. He likes stirring the pot a bit, providing some controversy. But not for the sake of controversy, but because questions need to be asked and answers sought which will move the church and individuals in it to higher heights in the Lord.

In this latest tome, Eyes Wide Open, Martin challenges some age-old beliefs that are truly of the Old Age, in order to bring his readers into the Age to come. The Old Covenant had glory, but it has faded, and has been ended…long ago, and we are to live in the Age to come, which is now, the time of the Kingdom of God which is ever growing and never ending, with a focus on the fulfillment of all things in Christ, not an escape from the world in which we live. This is a good read, filled with thought provoking and stirring information that is inspired by the Lord to help us grow in grace for God's glory.

Stan E. DeKoven, Ph.D., MFT
President
Vision International University

Introduction
Who this book is for?

I became a Christian over 30 years ago, around 18 years of age. I had quite a dramatic conversion experience, and no one would ever be able to convince me that God wasn't real or that Jesus was not the Son of God and savior of the world after that. I came to faith in Christ during the Charismatic Movement in the UK, and so I wasn't just a Christian, I was an "on fire" enthusiastic, passionate, "Spirit-filled" Christian.

That doesn't mean I was a Fundamentalist. I didn't even know what that meant. I was seeking to grow in my faith, in my personal relationship with God, in understanding scripture, discovering my God-given gifts and purpose, and becoming the kind of person God would want me to be. I didn't become a debater, or protestor, or professional arguer (thankfully, there were no social media then). My goal was to become a better person—more Christ-like. Maybe that's your goal too, and perhaps you find much of the Christian church and their response to things to be unhelpful and actually detrimental to you becoming more Christ-like. If so, you are one of the people this book was written for.

- If you are a Christian who feels that something is seriously wrong with much of modern-day Christianity, and your question is, "Where is the love, compassion and forgiveness?"

- If you are gaining more and more Biblical knowledge but somehow it just doesn't seem to fit—like you have all the pieces of a jigsaw puzzle but no picture to see how to put them all together.

- If you are a "spiritual-but-not-religious" seeker who finds Jesus and His message captivating but also sees the Christian Church as off-putting.

- If you are a pursuer of mysteries, secrets, and hidden things, and you feel that the Bible contains all kinds of hidden secrets that are ignored or overlooked or even unknown by religious people.

Then this book is for you.

On my spiritual journey as a Christian (and especially after I became a pastor and was able to observe the spiritual journeys of others), I became increasingly frustrated with four "spiritual diseases" that I knew were wrong but which were so prevalent in the Christian Church. I also became fascinated with two mysteries that I kept coming across in the Bible and in Christian history, but which I heard no one speak about. Little did I know that the two mysteries contained the cure for the four spiritual diseases!

The spiritual diseases are Legalism, Literalism, Futurism, and Dualism. We will look at each of these in detail. **The mysteries** are the Mazzaroth (the zodiac in the Bible) and the Ages (and the meaning of the phrase "the end of the Age" in the Bible).

Firstly, why are there zodiac constellations mentioned so often in the Bible?

For instance: *"Lift up your eyes and look to the heavens: Who created all these? He who brings out the starry host one by one and calls forth each of them by name. Because of his great power and mighty strength, not one of them is missing"* (Isaiah 40:26).

And here: *"Can you direct the movement of the stars—binding the cluster of the Pleiades or loosening the cords of Orion? Can you direct the constellations through the seasons or guide the Bear with her cubs across the heavens? Do you know the laws of the universe? Can you use them to regulate the earth?"* (Job 38:31-33).

Same here: *"And God said, "Let there be lights in the expanse of the sky to separate the day from the night, and let them serve as SIGNS to mark seasons and days and years, and let them be lights in the expanse of the sky to give light on the Earth." And it was so."* (Genesis 1:14-15).

And here: *"And there shall be SIGNS in the sun, and in the moon, and in the stars."* (Luke 21:25)

Likewise here: *"After Jesus was born in Bethlehem in Judea, during the time of King Herod, Magi from the east came to Jerusalem and asked, "Where is the one who has been born king of the Jews? We saw his star when it rose and have come to worship him."* (Matthew 2:1-2)

Also: *"The heavens declare the glory of God; the skies proclaim the work of his hands. Day after day they pour forth speech; night after night they reveal knowledge."* (Psalm 19:1-2)

and here: *"A great sign appeared in heaven: a woman clothed with the sun, with the moon under her feet and a crown of twelve stars on her head."* (Revelation 12:1)

These can be seen in many other places of the scripture.

Secondly, what is an "Age" and why does the Bible continually talk about "Ages" and "the end of the Age" as if the readers understand what period of time that means?

For instance: *"Surely I am with you always, to the very end of the AGE."* (Matthew 28:20)

Also: *"Anyone who speaks against the Holy Spirit will not be forgiven, either in this AGE or in the AGE to come."* (Matthew 12:32)

Same here: *"The harvest is the end of the AGE, and the harvesters are angels. As the weeds are pulled up and burned in the fire, so it will be at the end of the AGE."* (Matthew 13:39-40)

Likewise here: *"What will be the sign of your coming and of the end of the AGE?"* (Matthew 24:3)

Similarly: *"No one who has left home or wife or brothers or parents or children for the sake of the kingdom of God will fail to receive many times as much in this AGE and, in the AGE to come, eternal life."* (Luke 18:29-30)

As well here: *"We do, however, speak a message of wisdom among the mature, but not the wisdom of this AGE or of the rulers of this AGE... None of the rulers of this AGE understood it."* (1 Corinthians 3:6-8)

Same here: *"These things happened to them as examples and were written down as warnings for us, on whom the fulfillment of the AGES has come."* (1 Corinthians 10:11)

Also: *"[Christ was raised] far above all rule and authority, power and dominion, and every title that can be given, not only in the present AGE but also in the one to come."* (Ephesians 1:21)

And here: *"Just and true are your ways, King of the AGES."* (Revelation 15:3)

These can also be seen in many other places of the scripture.

When I discovered that both of those things were connected, that the Hebrews, along with the rest of the Ancient Near East (and most of the ancient world in general) had "Ages" as part of their calendar system (days, weeks, months, years, Ages) and that they used the zodiac constellations (called the Mazzaroth in Hebrew) along with the sun and moon, to calculate their **calendar**, and that each Hebrew month was aligned with one of the twelve constellations, and that each of their "Ages" (approx. 2,160 years) was also aligned with one of the 12 constellations, and that they KNEW when they were in the general time period of "the end of an Age", it felt like I was reading scripture again for the first time.

At first, this was just an interesting mystery to solve, but as I solved it, I saw how it affected the four "spiritual diseases" that I have mentioned. I saw how understanding the change of an Age, and also understanding the symbols and allegories that were common amongst the people of the Bible, enabled us to read scripture with the same "mindset" as the original hearers, and that was the final nail in the coffin for **Legalism** (because the Age of Law FULLY ended in AD 70), **Literalism** (because I was now reading their symbols the way THEY intended and used them), **Futurism** (because understanding when the "End of the Age" actually was, according to the ancient calendar, meant that we could stop pushing it off into our future), and **Dualism** (because much of our misunderstanding of "satan" and how much power "evil" has, is based on literalizing passages that the authors intended to be allegorical, and all the power of the devil was overthrown at the end of what was "the present evil Age" to the first Christians (Galatians 1:4).

We are going to start with the four spiritual diseases, then we will look at the Ages and the End of the Age at Jesus' time, and then we will see how they dovetail together, and how proper theology helps you live a freer, more fulfilling, and better life.

Part I:
"If the blind lead the blind, both will fall into a ditch"

—Jesus, *Matthew 15:14*

Chapter 1:
Eyes Wide Open

In Stanley Kubrick's classic movie, *Eyes Wide Shut*, Tom Cruise plays a doctor who almost accidentally stumbles across a secret society of very powerful people, whose gatherings involve bizarre ceremonies and rituals. The title of the movie suggests that we are walking around with our eyes "wide shut"—that even though we look, we don't see the signs that are all around us, pointing the way to this conspiracy, "hidden in plain sight".

What if we take that motif and apply it to scripture? What if we are reading the Bible and yet are totally blind to things that are right there in front of us, "hidden in plain sight"? What if we have been conditioned to "see" certain things in the Bible and miss other things? What if, to quote Jesus, our religious traditions have made God's Word to us of no effect in our lives?

What if we decided that there simply MUST be something more, something we have gotten wrong, or misunderstood, due to blind spots and preconceived ideas which we hold to? What if we became so aware of how contradictory and confusing many Christian beliefs are, and we realized that we must be misunderstanding something—something staring us right in the face, yet which we cannot see? What if we decided to "open our eyes wide" to look for this "something".

Not to look for minute clues to some great secret that no one else has seen, but to look for the idea or concept that is so big, so huge, so all-pervasive in the teachings of Jesus and scripture, that is staring us straight in the face, yet which we don't see because our perception is blinkered by our worldview. BUT once we see it—we see it everywhere! Once our eyes have been opened wide, they never close again. Once we have experienced a major "aha" moment and have seen the true meaning of things, we can no longer be duped by a half-baked tradition that tells us to see something else.

Let me quote something I wrote in a previous book*

"Most Christians, including those who hold to the popular end-time view, will claim that their beliefs are based solely on the teachings of the Bible. But every one of us— no matter how sincere we may be—bring to the Bible, not an empty mind, but a mind full of presuppositions, beliefs, views of reality, experiences and even political views, which influence the way we see things, and therefore, influence our interpretation of scripture. We look at the Bible through a lens of our culture, and therefore, we can misinterpret the Bible." (*Victorious Eschatology, by Harold Eberle and Martin Trench)

I have changed many of my beliefs and ideas over the years as I have tried to see things (including scripture) with an informed, yet propaganda-free mind (at least as much as I could manage to do). I was brought up in a nominally Christian home, and so I did have an awareness of God and of the most well-known Bible stories.

Then, in my late teens, after years of "wandering in the wilderness", I had a very dramatic and sudden conversion experience, and eventually became a pastor. So, I lived and ministered for many years within the charismatic section of Christianity, and I grew spiritually, I grew as a person, and I loved every minute of it all. I did flirt with more hard-core fundamentalism for a few years (once "Christian TV" came to the UK, we were exposed to all sorts of kooks and cranks from the sometimes wacky and angry world of televangelists). But I eventually could no longer accept the huge dichotomy between "pure doctrine" and the un-Christlike behavior and attitudes it seemed to produce. "A good tree bears good fruit, a bad tree bears bad fruit—you will know a tree by the fruit it produces", said Jesus.

As I began to doubt how good the fundamentalist tree was, I was also revisiting some of the history of Christianity that I had learned about when studying theology. I started to explore areas of theology that I hadn't given much time before (like eschatology). I also explored new expressions of church, learned to drop "Christianeze" and simply speak to people in the language they use, engage people from alternative spiritualities, continue my post-graduate studies, and study the early church fathers and revival movements throughout history.

Now, I could see it! I could see why we are all too often the opposite of what Jesus taught and exemplified. And this is not because I am a great detective—actually, the fact that it took me so long to see this bigger picture is a bit disturbing, and what I discovered was nothing new, so what I will write about in this book is nothing new and nothing that couldn't be discovered in many other books. But write it I must, because there are so many voices and books teaching a toxic version of Christianity and Jesus and faith that we need as many people as possible to be demonstrating genuine, authentic, holistic faith in a God of love, as revealed by Jesus.

As I looked at Jesus, His message and mission, through new eyes, it was like being "converted" all over again. I experienced a closeness with God, (a union with God), as a loving, forgiving, encouraging presence, and the Bible became a fresh—and far more interesting—book.

The truth is, (and everyone knows it), we have a big problem in the Christian church today. Whether it is Catholic sexual abuse scandals, congregations of "nice" people having to close their doors for lack of interest, congregations of "angry" people protesting everything, or pastors and theologians losing their job for "heresy" (which usually means a very minor disagreement), it is clear that things aren't healthy in Christianity. Now, not everything is toxic. There are many wonderful congregations, brilliant teachers, and amazing church projects. But we need more of the good stuff and less of the immature (and honestly, downright ungodly) stuff.

This book only reflects my journey of faith. Maybe you would identify different problems and different solutions, but these are how I see things, so I would like to invite you to come on a journey and see things through my eyes for a while. Maybe if we all did that a bit more, there would be less division amongst people of faith.

As I see it, there are four big problems present in the beliefs of many modern-day Christians, and those four false-beliefs produce a whole lot of wrong thinking and wrong behavior. They are almost like spiritual diseases which prevent a person (or church) from growing and maturing, while simultaneously convincing them that they already know everything and so don't need to grow. **They are Legalism, Futurism, Literalism, and Dualism.**

The problem with these subjects is that we are looking at them from the wrong time in history. Some of these things (like **Legalism)** come from reading the Bible and explaining the Christian faith through the lens of the Old Testament—the Old Covenant. But we don't live during the period of the Old Covenant—we are looking at things from the wrong side of the cross and resurrection.

Then there are things like **Literalism**—that's a modern-day, western phenomenon. We have lost so much in the area of idioms, symbols, figures of speech, and metaphor in our western world. Because of that, we tend to read the Bible as if it were a scientific treatise or an encyclopedia—it's not. It's a collection of books (divinely inspired documents to be sure) that express a number of different genres of literature. You would never read a songbook or a book of poems or a book of parables/allegorical stories as if they were speaking of literal historical happenings, so why do we read all of the Bible as if it's a scientific history book when it contains all those genres and more?

But I don't want to just point the finger at others (after all that is one of my complaints about present-day Christianity—it's too judgmental of others). What I want to do is remind us afresh of a vision that has at its core the true meaning of Jesus Christ and what He and His early followers originally intended—a dream that was drastically compromised by later generations of the professing church, but a dream that, if followed today, could and would lead to a better and brighter future—not only for the Christian faith, but for the world that all of us share, regardless of our beliefs.

When we see the world, God, others, and our own faith journey through the lenses of **Legalism, Futurism, Literalism, and Dualism**, it makes everything feel pessimistic and winding down—like we are close to the "end of the world" (which is why so many churches seem to focus on that issue). But when we realize that we have been looking through cloudy glasses, and we have seen things wrongly—it causes the clouds to clear up, and we discover that it's not the end of the world—it's the beginning of a whole new world!

CHAPTER 2:
LEGALISM

Much of the Christian church seems confused about which covenant we are in. While claiming to believe that God has made a "New Covenant" through Jesus Christ, and it is a covenant that reveals God as a God of love and grace, who freely forgives, at the same time, we go on about "God's Laws" and quote passages from the Old Testament to judge the lifestyles of people we don't approve of. Or we expect that EVERY-ONE who claims to believe in Jesus should all think the same, dress the same, look the same, like the same things, believe the same doctrines, and then stay that way for the rest of their lives and never change (never grow, mature, learn new ideas, or outgrow old ones).

I think that accepting a "system" of doctrine misses the whole point of a growing relationship with God. If I believe that I have all my beliefs "correct," then I have nothing new to learn and will simply spend the rest of my life "defending" those beliefs. If, on the other hand, I keep an open and enquiring mind and heart, I will be open to learning new things and tweaking my beliefs to fit the new evidence. I am much more interested in seeing people's lives transformed through continual growth than see them simply saying "amen" to a whole list of doctrines or acceptable lifestyle choices.

Everyone is at a different stage in their life and in their journey of faith, and so need to hear different things from God and from scripture than others do. It's this on-going journey of discovery that keeps faith alive and fresh. **Legalism** is when we reduce faith down to a formula of human behavior and doctrinal agreement, and then we make that the litmus test of true spirituality, and judge everyone accordingly. It's all about outward actions and statements of faith, (not true inner transformation).

When it comes to lifestyle choices, whether the topic is Halloween, drinking alcohol, Old Covenant food laws, dressing "modestly", or celebrating special holy days and festivals—it all misses the point. In fact, the people who were obsessed with that sort of thing were the ones who missed the Messiah! **Jesus followers were those who had open hearts and minds to new ideas.** Here is what the New Testament says about legalism:

COLOSSIANS 2:8-23

*Don't let anyone capture you with empty philosophies and high-sounding nonsense that come from human thinking and from the spiritual powers of this world, rather than from Christ. For in Christ lives all the fullness of God in a human body. So you also are complete through your union with Christ…. So don't let anyone condemn you for what you eat or drink, or for not celebrating certain holy days or new moon ceremonies or Sabbaths. For these rules are only shadows of the reality yet to come. And Christ himself is that reality. Don't let anyone condemn you by insisting on pious self-denial or the worship of angels, saying they have had visions about these things. Their sinful minds have made them proud, and they are not connected to Christ, the head of the body. For he holds the whole body together with its joints and ligaments, and it grows as God nourishes it. You have died with Christ, and he has set you free from the spiritual powers of this world. So why do you keep on following the rules of the world, such as, "Don't handle! Don't taste! Don't touch!"? Such rules **are mere human teachings** about things that deteriorate as we use them. These rules may seem wise because they require strong devotion, pious self-denial, and severe bodily discipline. But they provide no help in conquering a person's evil desires.*

GALATIANS 2:11-16

*When Peter came to Antioch, I had to oppose him to his face, for what he did was very wrong. When he first arrived, he ate with the Gentile believers, who were not circumcised. But afterward, when some friends of James came, Peter wouldn't eat with the Gentiles anymore. He was afraid of criticism from these people who insisted on the necessity of circumcision. As a result, other Jewish believers followed Peter's hypocrisy, and even Barnabas was led astray by their hypocrisy. When I saw that they were not following the truth of the gospel message, I said to Peter in front of all the others, "Since you, a Jew by birth, have **discarded the Jewish laws** and are living like a Gentile, why are you now trying to make these Gentiles follow the Jewish traditions? You and I are Jews by birth, not 'sinners' like the Gentiles. Yet we know that a person is made right with God by faith in Jesus Christ, not by obeying the law. And we have believed in Christ Jesus, so that we might be made right with God because of our faith in Christ, not because we have obeyed the law. For no one will ever be made right with God by obeying the law."*

GALATIANS 3:1-5

Oh, foolish Galatians! Who has cast an evil spell on you? For the meaning of Jesus Christ's death was made as clear to you as if you had seen a picture of his death on the cross. Let me ask you this one question: Did you receive the Holy Spirit by obeying the law of Moses? Of course not! You received the Spirit because you believed the message you heard about Christ. How foolish can you be? After starting your new lives in the Spirit, why are you now trying to become perfect by your own human effort? Have you experienced so much for nothing? Surely it was not in vain, was it? I ask you again, does God give you the Holy Spirit and work miracles among you because you obey the law? Of course not! It is because you believe the message you heard about Christ.

MATTHEW 15:1-20

*Some Pharisees and teachers of religious law now arrived from Jerusalem to see Jesus. They asked him, "Why do your disciples disobey our age-old tradition? For they ignore our tradition of ceremonial hand washing before they eat. "Jesus replied, "And why do you, by your traditions, violate the direct commandments of God? … you cancel the word of God for the sake of your own tradition. You hypocrites! Isaiah was right when he prophesied about you, for he wrote, 'These people honor me with their lips, but their hearts are far from me. Their worship is a farce, for **they teach man-made ideas** as commands from God.'" Then Jesus called to the crowd to come and hear. "Listen," he said, "and try to understand. It's not what goes into your mouth that defiles you; you are defiled by the words that come out of your mouth." Then the disciples came to him and asked, "Do you realize you offended the Pharisees by what you just said?" Jesus replied, "Every plant not planted by my heavenly Father will be up-rooted, so ignore them. They are blind guides leading the blind, and if one blind person guides another, they will both fall into a ditch." Then Peter said to Jesus, "Explain to us the parable that says people aren't defiled by what they eat." "Don't you understand yet?" Jesus asked. "Anything you eat passes through the stomach and then goes into the sewer. But the words you speak come from the heart—that's what defiles you. For from the heart come evil thoughts, murder, adultery, all sexual immorality, theft, lying, and slander. These are what defile you. Eating with unwashed hands will never defile you."*

CHAPTER 3:
FUTURISM

The term "Futurism" can mean a number of things. For example, people who study current trends in technology, politics and world events and use that to "predict" what new advances or changes will happen in the future, are called "Futurists". That's not what I mean by the term. I am speaking of Theological or Biblical Futurists—those who are awaiting a future fulfillment of Biblical prophecy.

Ask your average, Western Christian (and even a lot of people who aren't Christians) when the "Last Days" or the "End Times" spoken of in the Bible are supposed to take place, and the chances are you will be told "These are the Last Days, we are living in the End Times". Nothing could be further from the truth!

In previous generations, people in Western education were taught classical history. They knew about the Egyptian, Greek and Roman empires, and about the writings of ancient historians, like Josephus and Herodotus and Eusebius. When they read the prophecies of Daniel, about how a great empire would arise in Greece, and its ruler would conquer all the previous empires in the Mediterranean area, including Israel, and after his death his empire would be divided into four empires (see Daniel 8:8-12), they didn't start to scour the newspapers to see what political figure and events in their day might just fit the bill. They KNEW immediately that it was speaking of the Greek empire under Alexander the Great, and how his empire was divided between his four main generals after his death (Ptolemy in Egypt, Selecus in Syria, Lysimachus in Asia Minor, and Antigonus in Macedonia). They didn't instantly know that because they were unusual geniuses, but because they had been taught classical history.

Or when they read Jesus' prediction of Jerusalem being surrounded by armies that carry an eagle banner, and how these armies would invade and destroy the entire city and its temple, and that *"this generation will not pass away until ALL these things are fulfilled"* (see Matthew 24), they KNEW what it spoke of—the destruction of Jerusalem by the Roman armies in the war of AD 66-70. They knew that because they already knew classical history before they read the prophecy.

It would be like you already knowing the history of the American Civil War, then stumbling across a prophecy that was written decades before the war, but which accurately described it in minute detail. When you read such a prophecy, you would instantly recognize the similarities between it and the Civil War. But if you knew nothing about the American Civil War—not even that there was one, then you would find it very difficult to identify what the prophecy was speaking of. And if you believed the prophecy was true, you would start to search for things which sound slightly similar to the prophecy to see if it could apply to your day and age, (and probably even make a YouTube video about "the coming Civil War"—ignorant to the fact that the prophecy was fulfilled a long time ago).

When people in former generations read Biblical prophecies, they could see instantly (because of their knowledge of history) that many of these prophecies had already been fulfilled. Knowing that the prophecies of scripture had exact fulfillments that were documented in historical records, was a great source of strength to them. It strengthened their faith in the God who knows "the end from the beginning".

Today, it seems much different. Many people are so enamored with conspiracy theories and "last days" alerts that instead of strengthening their faith in the efficacy of Biblical prophecies, it is a disappointment to them! "You mean I won't see all these things fulfilled in my lifetime?

That is a big disappointment!" We seem totally enamored with Futurism, with catastrophic events in our lifetime or our near future.

We seem to forget the fact that the prophecies of Revelation say repeatedly that they would be fulfilled *"very soon"* (in fact, that's how the whole book starts in Revelation 1:1), or that Jesus said regarding His prophecy of a time of great tribulation in Judea, that *"this generation will not pass away before all these things are fulfilled"* (Matthew 24:34), or that Jesus said that *"everything that the prophets had spoken"* was to be fulfilled in the 1st century, not the 21st century (see Luke 21:22 & 24:44). Or, even more importantly, that "after" the fulfillment of Daniel's, Jesus', John's (and "all the prophets") words, we should not be expecting doom and gloom, but rather, a kingdom that grows and advances, and will eventually fill the earth with peace, prosperity, and the presence of God.

If you expect the world to get worse and worse, with terrible times ahead, it will lead your thoughts and emotions down one trail—usually a trail involving conspiracy theories and weird websites that post the most sensational (and always, unprovable) stories—often involving candidates for a global dictator known as the Antichrist (an idea taught nowhere in the Bible), and even in Ancient Aliens! I have heard it all, and I'm sure you have too. If, on the other hand, you believe that the "Last Days" are behind us, and we are now living in the "new days" of the New Covenant, the days of God's advancing Kingdom, then you will have an entirely different attitude to life, faith, God, and the world.

CHAPTER 4:
LITERALISM

Another misunderstanding of the Bible comes in the form of interpreting it in a wooden, overly-literalistic fashion, and believing that you are taking it "more seriously" by doing this. How often have you heard someone say, "I take the whole Bible literally"? Usually, they mean that they are taking it more seriously, more faithfully, more trustingly than those who don't "take the whole Bible literally". The truth is, no one takes "the whole Bible literally" and everyone "interprets" the Bible when they read it. I have yet to meet anyone who thinks that Jesus was an actual, literal "door", or a grape "vine", or an oil "lamp"; yet, Jesus said He was all three of those things (see John 10:9, 15:5, 8:12).

Of course, we don't take figures of speech "literally". We don't do it when we listen to someone during a conversation, and we don't do it when we read the Bible, and it is clear that something is meant to be a figure of speech. But what about all the times that it is NOT clear to us that something is intended as a figure of speech?

Because the Bible was written in a different language than we speak, within a different **culture**, at a different time in history, their figures of speech were not the same as ours. There are plenty of examples in the Bible of figures of speech which would only be noticed by someone who spoke that language, (Aramaic, Hebrew or Greek—depending on which part of the Bible and which ancient manuscripts), lived in that culture, and understood the idioms commonly employed.

In ancient Aramaic, there are many idioms and expressions and figures of speech that were common to the native speakers (and even are used today in many Aramaic speaking communities in the East) which we totally miss. For example, saying someone turned into "a pillar of salt" was (and still is in some places) an Aramaic figure of speech meaning "to die of a stroke" (or in some similar way, where the body goes stiff).

So, Lot's wife looked back at the burning city of Sodom and was so shocked by the destruction she saw that she took a hemorrhage to the brain and died. She didn't turn into a fairy-tale statue, made of pink Himalayan salt! You are free to believe that she turned into a Disney-like statue if you want, but I can't see how it helps your relationship with God, helps you lead others into faith in Christ, or makes the Bible more believable or attractive in any way.

Another example would be when God told "ravens" to feed Elijah, and they brought him food in the morning and the evening. Do you think it was actual birds who brought him the food? Yes, I know that all things are possible with God, but please think this through with me. It was during a terrible famine, very few people had food in that area (with the possible exception of nomadic tribes who travelled from place to place). Where were the birds getting this food from? Were they flying into people's homes and stealing their last meal from them? Is God a thief? And the hungry birds didn't eat it themselves, but dropped it off to Elijah before they fell out of the sky in starvation?

What do Aramaic scholars and historians say? They say that "ravens" actually means "Arabians"! More specifically, nomadic Arabians who wore black robes and were known locally as "ravens." God spoke to THEM and told THEM to bring food to Elijah every day. Maybe my faith is weaker than yours, but I find that story much more believable because I can have faith that God will speak to someone about blessing me in some way and meeting my needs, but my faith level isn't very high when it comes to asking God to send birds into my house with $50 bills in their beaks! These examples are simply from understanding the Aramaic language and culture. (I strongly recommend the writings of

Dr. George Lamsa and Dr. Rocco Errico for further evidence and lots more examples of the light that can be shed on the Bible by seeing it from its original culturally Aramaic perspective). The two Biblical stories I mentioned can be found in Genesis 19 and 1 Kings 17.

But, as well as **cultural** and language differences, there are also huge theological differences between the people who penned the scriptures, and that of many who read them today. That can be especially seen in one of the genres of literature used in the Bible—apocalyptic. Do you remember when the word "sick" meant one thing, that someone was actually sick or unwell? Then it changed and could also mean that something or someone is evil ("that terrorist is totally sick"), and then it could also mean that something is actually fantastic ("that rollercoaster was totally sick, let's do it again").

Words change their meaning over time. If a phrase is used in the Bible, the important thing is to understand what it meant to THEM, to the people who originally used it and read it—not what it might mean to us, today. Even the word "apocalyptic" has changed its meaning. We tend to think it means some terrible disaster, or war, or "the end of days", or we associate it with "apocalyptic movies" (usually starring Nicolas Cage). We now think that the term means "the catastrophic events of war and natural disasters that will accompany the end of the world", but someone living in Biblical times, (including John who wrote "the apocalypse" at the end of the Bible), would be totally bewildered by our understanding of the word.

The term "apocalypse" is simply a particular genre of religious writing. The word literally means "to unveil or to reveal". An "apocalypse" was a prophecy or prophetic vision or experience, which was written down, and which showed great sweeps of history (past, present, and future) in the form of symbolic images. There are apocalypses in the Bible—many parts of Daniel, Ezekiel, and Zechariah, for example, depict their historical prophecies in the form of symbols.

"Behold I saw a he-goat come from Greece ....." (Daniel 8) is actually saying, "Alexander the Great shall rise to power in Greece and conquer the previous empires". When a great city or an empire was about to be conquered or fall, it was often depicted as "the stars shall fall, the sun shall turn dark, the moon won't shine" etc.

They never meant that those things would literally happen in the sky. It would be like us saying someone got in a fight and "had his lights punched out"—it's a figure of speech, an idiom, a way of speaking that is not intended to be taken literally. I don't know anyone whose "lights" were literally "punched out" nor I have ever seen literal "cats and dogs" raining down from the sky, nor do I know anyone who actually "died" from lack of a cup of coffee, but we say and hear those kinds of things all the time, and nobody takes us literally.

When Isaiah prophesied that Babylon would fall to the Medes in 593BC, he used this idiomatic language: *"Behold, the day of the Lord comes, cruel, with wrath and fierce anger, to make the land a desolation and to destroy its sinners from it. For the stars of the heavens and their constellations will not give their light; the sun will be dark at its rising, and the moon will not shed its light."* (Isaiah 13:9-10).

This was a well-known figure of speech. The stars, sun, and moon going dark over a nation or falling over a nation was a common symbol which meant that the power and rule of that nation or city would fall and come to an end. Isaiah's' prophecy was fulfilled, but no stars actually fell from the sky, and the sun didn't stop shining…just like no actual animals fall to the ground when we say that its "raining cats and dogs".

To take that passage LITERALLY, we would need to say that the stars, sun, and moon did, in fact, stop giving their light in 593BC. But they didn't, and yet, Isaiah's prophecy came true, and Babylon did fall. Rather than boast about taking things "LITERALLY", let's take things SERIOUSLY—seriously enough to investigate them.

To take the whole Bible "literally" is to mistreat this sacred book. I don't take it literally; I take it far more seriously than that. I don't want to simply "believe it" as it reads in English, "literally", I actually want to **understand** it first, and to do that, I need to know what it would have meant to the original writers & speakers—in their context, in their time in history, in their culture, (not what I can twist it to mean to me, thousands of years, miles, and cultural differences away).

When we read the Bible that way, it produces a much more well-rounded understanding and provides a faith which is stable (and not given to the whims of "every wind of doctrine"; Ephesians 4:14). It becomes something steadfast and sure, upon which we can base our life's journey. Of course, God can illuminate a passage of scripture to us and speak straight into our lives, regardless of the context of the passage, but what I am talking about here is not "hearing from God" but rather "understanding scripture".

Let's look at a misunderstood passage that becomes clear once we understand the culture and **customs** of the Ancient Near East. This passage is found in Isaiah 14, and it is often used to claim that the devil was once an angel in heaven, maybe even the worship leader, who sinned against God and was thrown out. The only way to make the passage say that, is to ignore the **culture** and **customs** of the time, and also ignore the **context** of the passage, which clearly states at the beginning and again at the end of the prophecy that it is speaking about a mortal, human man:

VERSE 4:

"take up this taunt against the king of Babylon"—not against the devil or a fallen angel.

VERSES 18-21:

"All the kings of the nations lie in state. But you are cast out of your tomb…a corpse trampled underfoot…Prepare a place to slaughter his children for the sins of their ancestors…"

This is quite clearly a human being—the King of Babylon. And in between those verses, we have the actual prophecy where it even describes him:

He has invaded other lands
He has overthrown cities
He has acted violently
He has cut down the cedars of Lebanon
He will become weak
He will be killed
His empire will come to an end

So, why do people think it's about the devil? Two reasons:

Firstly, the King James translation of the Bible uses the word "Lucifer" and that name, though it originally means "morning star" or "Venus", became associated with the devil. The word doesn't appear in other translations because it isn't there in the original Hebrew nor the Greek Septuagint. The word comes from Latin, and for some unexplained reason, the translators of the King James Bible inserted the Latin word for "morning star" instead of just translating the Hebrew term as "morning star".

Secondly, the passage says the following about this person:

How you have fallen from heaven, morning star, son of the dawn!

You have been cast down to the earth, you who once laid low the nations!

You said in your heart, 'I will ascend to the heavens; I will raise my throne above the stars of God; I will sit enthroned on the mount of assembly, on the utmost heights of Mount Zaphon. I will ascend above the tops of the clouds; I will make myself like the Most High.'

In the early church, the great theologian, Origen of Alexandria suggested that this passage could be used in an **allegorical** sense to refer to the devil. Somehow or other, people began to take it to be **literally** about the devil. So, we have some phrases that sound like more than a mortal man—fallen from heaven—morning star—ascend above the tops of the clouds—make myself like the Most High. We will come back to those in a moment.

This passage is often tied in with another passage from **Ezekiel 28**, which it clearly says is about the King of Tyre (not the devil):

"The word of the Lord came to me: 'Son of man, say to the ruler of Tyre, "This is what the Sovereign Lord says: "In the pride of your heart you say, 'I am a god; I sit on the throne of a god in the heart of the seas.' But you are a mere mortal and not a god, though you think you are as wise as a god…. By your great skill in trading you have increased your wealth and because of your wealth your heart has grown proud."

This is quite clearly a mortal human man—the King of Tyre. But then it also contains this apparently otherworldly language:

You were in Eden, the garden of God; every precious stone adorned you…You were anointed as a guardian cherub, for so I ordained you. You were on the holy mount of God; you walked among the fiery stones… Through your widespread trade you were filled with violence, and you sinned…I made a spectacle of you before kings. By your many sins and dishonest trade you have desecrated your sanctuaries.

So, when we combine those two passages, which themselves say quite clearly that they are about two Near-Eastern kings (Babylon and Tyre), we are left with some language which we don't really understand. If we take it "literally," then we have to conclude that it is talking about some supernatural being, but to do that, we have to ignore the fact that those passages say they are about mortal human kings. The phrases in question are:

Fallen from heaven
Called yourself a god
Wanted to ascend above clouds and stars
Wanted to sit on God's throne
Was in the garden of God
Walked amongst fiery stones
Was the anointed guardian cherub

Once we understand the **culture and customs** of the Ancient Near East, this is easily understood. When an ancient king, emperor or pharaoh (and even many of the Roman Caesars) was crowned as king, they were anointed and given the names of stars or gods or heavenly beings. It was believed that the kings were the descendants of gods and they would become stars upon their death. Many of the Pharaohs of Egypt were given the title, "morning star and evening star". It was also common to build temples and sanctuaries that were ziggurats (stepped pyramids) in the belief that the closer you could get to the clouds, the closer to the gods, (remember the Tower of Babel?). In their temples, they often used fire pits and fire altars, and so only the priests and the king walked among the stones of fire. Often, the king's palace would have a "garden of the gods" attached to it, and the king was supposed to "tend" to the garden as a way of communing with the heavens and receiving divine inspiration.

These passages are talking about how the Kings of Babylon and Tyre had taken on divine names and were supposed to fulfill divine purposes, but instead, they had become greedy, proud, violent, and so, they would be overthrown and would lose their kingdoms. And those prophecies were fulfilled. Let's strive to genuinely UNDERSTAND what the Bible is saying first, and let's not rip passages completely out of their context.

Here is one more example of the need to read in **context** and also to understand **culture** and **customs:** the concept of women wearing head-coverings when publicly praying or prophesying. The apostle Paul tells us that *"any woman who prays or prophesies with her head uncovered, dishonors her head"* (1 Corinthians 11:5). There are many legalistic churches which teach that this should be adopted literally, because, after all, the "Bible clearly says it". But it's one thing to simply read words and obey, it's quite another thing to actually *understand* those words, (in their original context), and then apply them.

Paul was speaking to a **culture** where unmarried women covered their heads with a particular head covering that everyone knew meant "I am not yet married, and I live with my parents, and my father is the 'head' of our home". If a man was interested in or attracted to that woman, he would know that he has to first ask her father. Women who were married also wore a head covering, which said to everyone who saw them "I am a married woman, and my husband is the 'head' of my home". She was not available for the interests of other men.

Among the Christians in Corinth, it seems that some women were abandoning their head coverings (perhaps because they had heard that "there is neither male nor female in Christ, we are all one" Galatians 3:28). This was causing problems. People were coming into Christian gatherings, and they thought that the women with no head coverings were "freely available" for any propositions (because that's what no head coverings meant in that culture). This was especially causing issues to travelling teachers, or "messengers" as they were called (some translations say "angels"—aggelos in Greek = "messengers"). Paul even admits that this was a **"custom"** (verse 16).

Now that we understand the context, we can "apply" it to our day—our equivalent would be wedding rings. Imagine if all the women in your church stopped wearing wedding rings, and single men thought the women were single too and began to propose to them, much to the anger of the women's husbands. Now, we have a true understanding and a modern day application.

Literalism and Legalism don't even care to understand what the passage is actually about.

CHAPTER 5:
DUALISM

This is where superstition sometimes crawls into the Christian faith. Dualism is basically the belief that there are two opposing forces in the universe—one good and one evil. It comes from Gnosticism and similar spiritual traditions (including Zoroastrianism), and it is able to appeal to certain Bible passages which makes it sound Biblical, but the overall view of God, creation, and humanity is definitely not Biblical.

The Biblical picture is that there is *one God* who created all things and whose presence fills all things, and He is a good God—God of love and light. Dualism teaches that there is a constant conflict between the physical universe (which is evil, or at least "fallen" and negative) and the spiritual world (which is good and pure); that means our bodies, our natural appetites, and all things physical are bad, but everything spiritual is good. Secular music and movies are bad, but Christian music and movies are good! (Seriously, I find that it is often the very reverse of that). Worshipping God in church is good, but going to a sports game and cheering for your team is worldly, secular, unspiritual, and sinful.

Dualism is basically the belief that evil and good exist in equal proportions—God and Satan, or the Kingdom and a "fallen, sinful" world. Many people would claim that they don't believe that, and even have it in their statements of faith that they believe that God is supreme, etc. But the way they pray, preach, and interpret scripture implies that they believe that "Satan has been tempting me all week" and "we need to pray against the powers of darkness" and "we are in a culture war with the world" all shows that their true worldview is dualistic.

- To believe that the whole planet is a "fallen creation" and that God's people are a remnant who are fighting to redeem it, is dualism, (the Bible only says that humans "fall" when we sin— *"all have sinned and have fallen..."* Romans 3:23—not that creation or animals are fallen or evil).

- To believe that our bodies are "fallen and sinful" but our spirits are good and righteous is dualism (our whole being— spirit/mind/body are good and created in God's image).

- To believe that Satan is "alive and well on planet earth" is dualism as satan is defeated, dethroned, bound, and stripped.

- To believe that satan or demons have control over physical creation (like weather) is dualism. *("the earth is the Lord's and everything in it"*; Psalm 24:1)

It was dualism that was referred to in the Bible as "the spirit of antichrist". It may surprise you to discover that the word "antichrist" is only used in two places in the Bible—in the first letter of John and in his second letter (never by Jesus, nor by Paul, nor in Revelation). From early church history, we discover that in John's day, after his release from imprisonment on the island of Patmos (where he wrote the Book of Revelation), he returned to the city of Ephesus, only to discover that in his absence, a false teacher named Cerinthus had been spreading a form of Gnosticism that was a mixture of Dualism and Legalism.

The dualistic part said that physical matter is evil; therefore, Christ could not have "come in the flesh" but must have only "appeared" to have done so. Cerinthus' answer was to say that Jesus was a normal human being, conceived in the normal way, with nothing divine about Him, but He became a "channeller" for a spirit being called "the Christ" who entered Him at His baptism and left Him on the cross. "Jesus" and "the Christ" were two different beings, so "Jesus Christ did not come in the flesh". To this new doctrine, John was very clear, and take special note of these verses, BECAUSE THESE ARE THE ONLY VERSES IN THE BIBLE THAT EVEN MENTION THE WORD "ANTI-CHRIST"—

1 JOHN 2:18-23 & 4:2-4 & 2 JOHN 7-8

Dear children, the last hour is here. You have heard that antichrist is coming, and already many such antichrists have appeared. From this we know that the last hour has come. These people left our churches, but they never really belonged with us; otherwise they would have stayed with us. When they left, it proved that they did not belong with us. But you are not like that, for the Holy One has given you his Spirit, and all of you know the truth. So I am writing to you not because you don't know the truth but because you know the difference between truth and lies. And who is a liar? Anyone who says that Jesus is not the Christ. Anyone who denies the Father and the Son is an antichrist. Anyone who denies the Son doesn't have the Father, either. But anyone who acknowledges the Son has the Father also......

This is how we know if they have the Spirit of God: If a person claiming to be a prophet acknowledges that Jesus Christ came in a real body, that person has the Spirit of God. But if someone claims to be a prophet and does not acknowledge the truth about Jesus, that person is not from God. Such a person has the spirit of antichrist, which you heard is coming into the world and indeed is already here. But you belong to God, my dear children. You have already won a victory over those people, because the Spirit who lives in you is greater than the spirit who lives in the world...

Many deceivers have gone out into the world. They deny that Jesus Christ came in a real body. Such a person is a deceiver and an antichrist. Watch out that you do not lose what we have worked so hard to achieve. Be diligent so that you receive your full reward.

There is one creative power present in the universe, *"I am the Lord, and besides me there is NO OTHER"* (Isaiah 45:5), and all sin has already been atoned for in full, and all the powers of evil are defeated. Evil springs from the heart of man not from a secondary evil deity (James 1:14). That doesn't mean that sin doesn't exist (it does), or that evil spirits don't exist (they do), or that we can't be led away from sincere devotion to God (because we can), or that we can't be tempted (because we regularly are). But it IS to say that the devil and all his cohorts are like ants compared to the one true God; that where sin abounds, grace does much more abound; that God is love. He HAS many attributes, but He IS love. God is light, and in Him there is no darkness at all (1 John 1:5; 4:8).

With regard to the physical creation, we are not supposed to shun it or withdraw from it, but rather, we are to enjoy it and live our lives to the full:

ECCLESIASTES 2:24

So I decided there is nothing better than to enjoy food and drink and to find satisfaction in work. Then I realized that these pleasures are from the hand of God.

Now, it is true that we can simply look at each of these "four diseases", as we have done above, and prove them to be wrong simply by examining scripture on each point. We can look at passages that clearly teach that we are saved by a free gift of God's grace and that nothing we can do can add to that work (Ephesians 2:8-9), or we can look and see that "All authority in heaven and on earth" has been given to Jesus (Matthew 28:18) which effectively means the devil has none. But the fact that so many of the passages in the New Testament which deal with these four issues also mention the mysterious "Ages", shows that there must be a connection, that there is something more, something far bigger and so neglected that most Christians today are unaware of it, and yet it provides the final nail in the coffin for those "diseases" and shows that Jesus birth, life, ministry, death, resurrection, ascension, sending of the Spirit, and fulfilled prophecy was such a cosmic turning point, that there is no going back and mixing now-discarded Old Covenant perspectives with the new age that Jesus ushered in. That's what we will look at next.

Part 2:
"How can you not interpret the signs of the times?"

—Jesus, *Matthew 16:3*

CHAPTER 6:
THE "SIGNS" OF THE TIMES

MATTHEW 16:2-3

Jesus answered them, "When it is evening, you say, 'It will be fair weather, for the sky is red.' And in the morning, 'It will be stormy today, for the sky is red and threatening.' You know how to interpret the appearance of the sky, but you cannot interpret the signs of the times.

I mentioned in my Introduction that I began to notice two mysteries in the Bible that I heard no one talk about, and so I had to research through old books and theological tomes, as well as study more deeply about church history and the Ancient Near-Eastern culture. I kept noticing that where the old King James translation of the Bible referred to "the end of the world" (e.g., Matthew 24:3 and 28:20), all modern translations and all "literal" translations said "the end of the Age". So, what are those passages talking about? The end of the world, or the end of an Age? And if an Age, what does that even mean?

As I listened to sermons and podcasts and read Christian literature, I noticed that the people who used the translations with the phrase "end of the world" tended to suppose that those passages were, in fact, about the end of the world, and so they attempted to "interpret" everything else in those passages to "fit" that scenario. The world is obviously still here, so, they presume, those passages haven't been fulfilled yet—they are awaiting fulfilment. I also noticed that people who used the translations which said "end of the Age" tended to interpret them in a different way to the "end of the world" people. The more research I did, the more I discovered that every theological examination of those passages that actually analyzed the original languages and wording, all said that the correct translation was "Age" and not "world" (regardless of their denominational or theological background).

At the same time, I frequently noticed that the Bible contains a lot of zodiac imagery. I thought Christians were supposed to be against all that stuff? As I researched these zodiac signs in scripture, I discovered that Horoscopes (which are criticized in the Bible; Isaiah 37:13-14) were the Babylonian take on the zodiac signs, seeking to use them as "personal prophecy", whereas other Ancient Near-Eastern cultures saw them as a "cosmic prophecy"—a story in the sky for all humanity, (not for personal guidance).

It wasn't until I read the works of Rev. Gordon Strachan that I realized that, in their calendar, each zodiac sign lasted for an Age! The two mysteries were one and the same—one using regular language ("Age" and "end of the Age"), and the other using symbolic language (Age of Aires, Age of Pisces, etc.). Both the passages in the scripture that speak of the "end of the Age" and the ancient meaning of the 12 signs of the zodiac, pointed to the same thing—the event which would transform human history—the end of one Age (and the Old Covenant) and the beginning of a new Age (and New Covenant which would continue on through all succeeding Ages).

We tend to focus on the Big Events in the Bible (creation, the flood, the Exodus, the cross & resurrection, etc.) but what we tend to overlook, is God's plan throughout human history, and how His plan is progressive, develops over time, and has a purpose. We need to know where we live in God's plan and differentiate that from when others lived. We are going to look at what the Bible means when it speaks of "Ages", what an Age is and what the "end of the Age" means, and how the apocalyptic passages in the Bible use zodiac constellations to speak about Ages and their ending.

God has a long and progressive plan that He is working out, and a major cosmic change took place at the "End of the (Old Covenant) Age" when the New Testament was being written. For example, we don't live under the Old Covenant or the Mosaic Law. We live under a New and Better Covenant under the grace of Jesus Christ:

JOHN 1:17

The law was given through Moses; but grace and truth came through Jesus Christ.

HEBREWS 8:6-13

*Jesus, our High Priest, has been given a ministry that is far superior to the old priesthood, for he is the one who mediates for us a far **better covenant** with God, based on better promises. If the first covenant had been faultless, there would have been no need for a second covenant to replace it. But when God found fault with the people, he said: "The day is coming, says the Lord, when I will make **a new covenant** with the people of Israel and Judah. This covenant **will not be like the one I made** with their ancestors when I took them by the hand and led them out of the land of Egypt. They did not remain faithful to my covenant, so I turned my back on them, says the Lord. But this is the new covenant I will make with the people of Israel on that day, says the Lord: I will put my laws in their minds, and I will write them on their hearts. I will be their God, and they will be my people. And they will not need to teach their neighbors, nor will they need to teach their relatives, saying, 'You should know the Lord.' For everyone, from the least to the greatest, will know me already. And I will forgive their wickedness, and I will never again remember their sins." When God speaks of a "new" covenant, it means he has made **the first one obsolete**. It is now out of date **and will soon disappear**.*

God's plan has always been progressing. He is working towards a goal, an end-game:

EPHESIANS 1:9-11

God has now revealed to us his **mysterious** *will regarding Christ—which is to fulfill his own good plan.* **And this is the plan:** *At the right time he will bring everything together under the authority of Christ—everything in heaven and on earth. Furthermore, because we are united with Christ, we have received an inheritance from God, for he chose us in advance, and he makes everything work out according to his plan.*

CHAPTER 7:
THE LAST DAYS ARE NOW THE PAST DAYS.

I get very weary of all the "end time" predictions that go on in the name of Jesus. You would think that if someone wanted to dedicate their lives to spreading the message of the "Last Days" and of the "End Times", that they would have at least taken the time to find out what those terms actually mean. The truth is, people seem to read what the Bible says about "the Last Days", and somehow or other, without actually researching what that term meant to the people who used it in the first century, simply presume that it must be talking about the day and age that we live in. "Do you think we are in the Last Days?" "Well, that's just a sign that we are in the End Times", or "the Bible did predict that such wars/tsunamis/whatever would happen at the End—these things will just get worse because we are in the Last Days and the End Times are upon us"... I read that kind of propaganda ALL THE TIME online.

But why do the people making these comments automatically presume that the "Last Days" and the "End Times" are speaking about OUR day and age? Why would they not actually do some research into what those phrases originally meant? I simply can't answer that. I am an inquisitive person. I want to find out exactly what something means before I throw my lot in with it. So, let me share the conclusion of the more than 15 years of research that I've done on this topic. Then I'll show you how I arrived at this conclusion.

We do NOT Live in the Last Days. These are NOT the End Times. When the Bible speaks of the "End Times", it is ALWAYS speaking about the "End of the Age"—not the end of the world. It's not the world or planet earth that is coming to an "End" in those Biblical passages—it's an "Age", (so we need to find out what an "Age" is).

It is easy to prove that this is true. I would challenge anyone to go through every New Testament reference to "the Last Days" and read it in context. You will make a startling discovery. *Every passage* says that Jesus and the first apostles, and early Christians in the first century AD, lived in the "Last Days'. THEY lived in the "Last Days", not us. For us, **the Last Days are the past days.** Let me show you that:

HEBREWS 1:1 – JESUS TEACHING MINISTRY TOOK PLACE DURING "THE LAST DAYS"

*"Long ago God spoke many times and in many ways to our ancestors through the prophets. But now, **in these last days**, he has spoken to us through his Son".*

I PETER 1:20 – JESUS DEATH TOOK PLACE DURING "THE LAST DAYS"

*"God chose Jesus as your ransom long before the world began, but now **in these last days** he has been revealed for your sake".*

ACTS 2:17 – PENTECOST HAPPENED IN "THE LAST DAYS"

*Peter said: What you see was predicted long ago by the prophet Joel: 'In **the last days**,' God says, 'I will pour out my Spirit upon all people."*

2 Timothy 3:1 – Timothy needed to know that he would be experiencing difficult times in the "last days" because he was living in them

"You should know this, Timothy, that in **the last days** *there will be very difficult times."*

James 5:3-4 – James warns people in his time, the "last days" were upon them.

Your gold and silver are corroded. Their corrosion will testify against you and eat your flesh like fire. You have hoarded wealth **in the last days***. Look! The wages you failed to pay the workers who mowed your fields are crying out against you. The cries of the harvesters have reached the ears of the Lord Almighty.*

Jude v17-19 – Jude said that the "last days" scoffers lived in his day.

But, dear friends, remember what the apostles of our Lord Jesus Christ foretold. They said to you, **"In the last days** *there will be scoffers who will follow their own ungodly desires." These are the people who divide you, who follow mere natural instincts and do not have the Spirit.*

1 JOHN 2:18 – JOHN WROTE THIS WHEN HE WAS THE LAST REMAINING MEMBER OF THE 12 DISCIPLES, AND BY THAT TIME IT WASN'T JUST THE "LAST DAYS", IT WAS THE "LAST HOUR"!

*Dear children, this is **the last hour***; *and as you have heard that antichrist is coming, even now many antichrists have come. This is how we know it is **the last hour.***

All of these passages make it clear that THEY were living in the "Last Days", not us. So, the Last Days of what? Of the "Age"—the one that was coming to an end in their lifetime, the period that is called the "Last Days" is also referred to as the "End of the Age", and Jesus Himself predicted that the Age would End within one generation:

"When will these things happen? And what will be the sign of your coming and of the End of the Age", asked Jesus' disciples, when He had predicted that the Temple in Jerusalem would be destroyed. He answered, *"This generation will not pass away before all these things are accomplished"* (Matthew 24:1-3, 34).

The "End of the Age" was going to happen within one generation of Jesus' prediction, and the people who lived during that final generation were living in the "Last Days" of that "Age" which was coming to an "End".

And what "Age" was that, which was coming to an "End"? **It was the Old Covenant Age.** From the time of Abraham to the time of Jesus, the descendants of Abraham had lived under a Covenant with God. That Covenant was to last for an "Age". The prophets sent to Israel predicted that when that Covenant came to an End, there would be a "New Covenant", and there would be a "Kingdom" which would expand and increase, "without end". Jesus' disciples were brought up in a culture and religion which understood these concepts, and so when Jesus predicted that the Temple would be destroyed in the lifetime of the disciples, they realized that this would be the "End of the Age", and so they asked for some clarity about when the "End of the Age" would be.

Let's look at some scripture passages which show this. A "literal" translation of the Bible (one which translates it word-by-word and sticks to the closest English word to the original Greek, Hebrew, and Aramaic words, regardless of whether it "flows" well or not) may be a bit sticky to read, but it is good for detailed study. I will be ensuring that the correct terms are used in the quotations I give, and you can check them all out in a literal translation (like Young's Literal Translation), to see that for yourself. So, here we go:

GENESIS 17:8

I have given to you, and to your descendants after you, the land of your sojourning, the whole land of Canaan, for an **age-enduring possession**, *and I have become their God.*

Note: God did NOT give the "promised land" of Canaan to Abraham and his descendants for an "everlasting" possession, as some English translations suggest. The exact, actual word is for an "Age-enduring" possession. There was going to be a whole Age where Abraham's descendants would inherit that land—for a purpose—for the purpose of preparing a culture and society that would bring forth the Messiah who would usher in a New Covenant and a New Age, the One who would bring forgiveness for all people and a whole new era that would start small but would grow and develop and spread until the world is filled with blessing, grace, and the Kingdom of God.

The point is, God promised that Abraham and his descendants would inherit that land "for an Age-enduring possession". Then, the prophets started to come along and show what the "next Age" would have in store, what would happen AFTER this "Age" was over and this Covenant was fulfilled:

JEREMIAH 31:31-34

The day is coming," says the Lord, "when I will make a new covenant with the people of Israel and Judah. This covenant will not be like the one I made with their ancestors when I took them by the hand and brought them out of the land of Egypt. They broke that covenant, though I loved them as a husband loves his wife," says the Lord. "But this is the new covenant I will make with the people of Israel after those days," says the Lord. "I will put my instructions deep within them, and I will write them on their hearts. I will be their God, and they will be my people. And they will not need to teach their neighbors, nor will they need to teach their relatives, saying, 'You should know the Lord.' For everyone, from the least to the greatest, will know me already," says the Lord. "And I will forgive their wickedness, and I will never again remember their sins."

EZEKIEL 36:25-27

Then I will sprinkle clean water on you, and you shall be clean; I will cleanse you from all your filthiness and from all your idols. I will give you a new heart and put a new spirit within you; I will take the heart of stone out of your flesh and give you a heart of flesh. I will put My Spirit within you and cause you to walk in My statutes

So, the people of Israel were aware that their covenant was to last "an Age" and that they would inhabit the land during that time, and that God had promised to make a New Covenant, but they weren't so clear about what would happen to the Old Covenant, and Temple, and Land, and Law. But then Jesus came along and predicted that *"the blood of all the righteous prophets will be held to the account of THIS generation"*, and as a result, their *"House will be left desolate"* (see Matthew 23:31-39)—not our generation, but the generation He was speaking to. Then His disciples, (who knew that the reference to "your House shall be left desolate" meant the Temple in Jerusalem being destroyed) asked Him, *"When will these things be? And what shall be the sign of your coming and of the End of the Age?"* (Matthew 24:3).

Then Jesus answered them, giving them many warning signs about what was going to happen and how THEY would see these things (not us—we wouldn't see them, except by looking back at it as history, but THEY—Jesus' disciples—the people to whom He was speaking—would see these things) and how "this generation will not pass away until all these things are fulfilled" (Matt. 24:34). The disciples would be living in the "Last Days" at the "End" of the Old Covenant "Age". THEY would witness the "End of the Age" and it would happen within "this generation" that Jesus was addressing at that time.

In the Bible, a generation is usually regarded as about 40 years (they walked in the wilderness for 40 years until that generation had died; see Numbers 32:13). So, if Jesus spoke that prophecy around 30 AD, then He only had until 70 AD for it to come to pass, and so it did, (as we shall see).

The New Covenant had arrived in Jesus and was "ratified" by His death and resurrection, but it was still in its infancy—it was like the sun beginning to "rise" early in the morning when it is still dark, and the moon (Old Covenant) is still visible. There is a period of time when the sun is "ascending" and the moon is "descending" and both are in the sky at the same time. So, the New Covenant was "ascending" and the Old Covenant was "descending", but for a period of time—a Transition Period, theologians call it—both were still "visible" and existed "side by side"—the Old Covenant did not *fully* pass away at the cross—it was rendered "obsolete" at the cross but it continued for "one generation" or for the "Last Days of the Old Covenant Age"—with the Temple, sacrifices, and priesthood still in place and "visible" in Jerusalem—but it was dying out; it was soon to disappear.

So, the author of Hebrews wrote that the New Covenant had arrived, and the Old Covenant was now obsolete, but it had not yet passed away, and it would "soon pass away", and so it did—in AD 70—"one generation" after Jesus' prediction, following the fulfillment of all the warning "signs" He told His disciples they would see; "Jerusalem surrounded by armies" as the Romans invaded, destroyed the city, razed the Temple to the ground, fulfilling Jesus' prophecy that "not one stone would be left upon another". The Old Covenant, and all its accoutrements (Temple, priesthood, sacrifices, Law) fully and finally "disappeared" out of view and fully "passed away".

HEBREWS 8:13

By calling this covenant "new," he has made the first one obsolete; and what is obsolete and outdated **will soon disappear***.*

Let's just have a look at Jesus' prediction of the end of the Age and when it would happen. We find Jesus' Olivet Discourse (His prophetic speech to His disciples on the Mount of Olives) in three of the gospels (Matthew, Mark and Luke) but it is well captured in Matthew from chapter 23-25. So many people have thought that Jesus' prophecy of a time of tribulation, wars and rumors of wars, earthquakes and famines are all about "the end of the world" and so look for confirming events in our day that may line up with the prophecy. However, once you read it in its actual context, you see that it says NOTHING about the day and age that we live in, nor about "the End of the world", nor any of the popular images that people superimpose upon it.

We will see—if we simply read it in context—that it is a prophecy of a time of trouble and tribulation which would come upon Judea (not the whole world), within the lifetime of the disciples who were listening (not our lifetime), at the hands of invading Roman armies (not the "Antichrist"), and it would result in the final end of the Temple in

Jerusalem (not the end of planet earth), and this would be the end of the Old Covenant Age (not the end of the world). If THAT is what this prophecy of Jesus actually says, in its original context, (and, as we shall see, it is), then a whole lot of sermons, books, and poorly made movies about the "End Times" should be taken to the nearest dumpster.

So, why is it so obscure? Why would the authors of the Bible not make it clearer? Well, clearer to whom? It was apparent to them and to their hearers/readers. They were very familiar with the meaning of the terms "Age" and "Age-enduring", and so they never stop to explain exactly WHAT they mean by those terms, because their readers KNEW what those terms meant.

By way of analogy, imagine that in 2,000 years' time, some archeologists came across some references made by two people in OUR day, in which they mention "Facebook". Those people would never explain WHAT Facebook is to each other because they both know what it is. But to the archeologists in 2,000 years' time, "Facebook" might be a total mystery! Even if they look up the dictionary definitions of "face" and "book", they would be none the wiser. In fact, the dictionary definition would take them completely in the wrong direction. Their task would NOT be to work out what people in our time were talking about by using THEIR dictionary definitions of "face" and "book", but rather, to do some research to find out what WE were talking about when we used that term.

Likewise, the term "Age" could mean lots of things to us ("this day and age", the "middle ages", the "Bronze Age", etc.). But our task is NOT to superimpose our own modern-day definition of the words "Age" and "Age-enduring" onto the Bible, but to find out what THEY meant by those terms—terms which were used so commonly in that time that no explanation was needed. As we shall see later on, the term "Age" was connected to their calendar, (it was a specific period of time which they could calculate) and there are a whole series of "Ages" mentioned in the

Bible. However, let's start by simply looking at the two Ages we have mentioned already (the End of the Old Covenant Age during the "Last Days" and the beginning of the New Covenant Age) and how they relate to Jesus' prediction in His Olivet Prophecy where He explained what would happen within one generation.

CHAPTER 8:
THE OLIVET PROPHECY

In Matthew 23, Jesus is speaking to and about the religious leaders of His day (Pharisees, Sadducees, scribes, and teachers of the Law). He isn't happy with them. They have replaced a relationship with God and compassion for people with a strict and harsh religious attitude. It doesn't start off well:

"Woe to you, teachers of the law and Pharisees, you hypocrites! You shut the door of the kingdom of heaven in people's faces. You yourselves do not enter, nor will you let those enter who are trying to." (Matthew 23:13).

And He keeps going—seven times. Woe after woe. They are legalistic, greedy, unkind, and harsh. And He concludes chapter 23 with these words:

"You snakes! You brood of vipers! How will you escape being condemned to *Gehenna? Therefore I am sending you prophets and sages and teachers. Some of them you will kill and crucify; others you will flog in your synagogues and pursue from town to town. And so upon YOU will come all the righteous blood that has been shed on earth, from the blood of righteous Abel to the blood of Zechariah son of Berekiah, whom you murdered between the temple and the altar. Truly I tell you, ALL THIS WILL COME UPON THIS GENERATION. Jerusalem, Jerusalem, you who kill the prophets and stone those sent to you, how often I have longed to gather your children together, as a hen gathers her chicks under her wings, and you were not willing. Look, your house is left to you desolate. For I tell you, you will not see me again until you say, 'Blessed is he who comes in the name of the Lord." (Matthew 23:33-39)

[*Gehenna was the burning landfill site outside of Jerusalem where the Jews threw their garbage, and where the Romans would throw the bodies of everyone in Jerusalem that they would slaughter in the coming war of AD 66-70].

The disciples were shocked that Jesus had said the Temple would be overthrown ("your House shall be left desolate"; Matthew 23:38), and so they pointed out to Jesus how amazing the architecture of the Temple was:

Jesus left the temple and was walking away when his disciples came up to him to call his attention to its buildings. *"Do you see all these things?"* he asked. *"Truly I tell you, not one stone here will be left on another; every one will be thrown down."* (Matthew 24:1-2).

He confirmed that what He had said, He meant. The Temple would be destroyed—the symbol of the Old Covenant would come to a full end. The disciples knew that could only mean one thing—the end of the Age, so as they continued walking down the hill from Jerusalem, and back up the opposite hill of the Mount of Olives, (where they would have a direct view of the Temple) they asked for more information:

As Jesus was sitting on the Mount of Olives, the disciples came to him privately. "Tell us," they said, "when will this happen, and what will be the sign of your coming and of the end of the Age?" (Matthew 24:3)

Because one or two English translations incorrectly say "end of the world" there, many people presume that they are asking about Jesus second coming and the final judgment. However, Jesus had not even indicated anything about His second coming to them. Instead, Jesus lays out a three-part plan:

1. Within one generation, the Romans would invade Jerusalem and destroy the city and the Temple. There would be warning signs before this happened—small nations would begin to rebel against the Roman empire and there would be wars and rumors of wars; there would be earthquakes and famines (all of which happened during that 40-year-period around the Mediterranean area, some of the earthquakes and famines are even mentioned in the New Testament: Matthew 28:2 and Acts 11:28) and finally, they would see "eagles" surrounding the city (the Roman eagle banners). At that point, they were to flee the city to the mountains. And so they did. History tells us that the believers in Jesus fled Jerusalem when they saw the fulfillment of Jesus' prophecies and went to the mountain area of Pella. (Matthew 24)

2. Then, there would be a long period of time when the gospel is going forth and (it seems) that the Bridegroom is delayed in His coming, and during that period of time, our job is to discover our God-given gifts and put them to fruitful use, as we will be called upon to give an account of what we have done with our lives, one day (Matthew 25:1-30).

3. Then, there will be a final return of Christ and a final judgment, but with no warning signs, unlike the tribulation that would happen within a generation. (Matthew 25:31-46).

[For a full, verse-by-verse description of what each of Jesus statements means and how they were fulfilled, see *Victorious Eschatology* by Martin Trench and Harold Eberle]

So, it wasn't the "End of the World" that Jesus was predicting—it was the end of the world AS THEY KNEW IT—the End of the Age.

CHAPTER 9:
REVELATION GENERATION

Which generation was the Book of Revelation written to?

Many people would answer with "our generation" or "the final generation". But which generation does the book itself say it is written to?

The Book of Revelation is the last book in the New Testament. Its actual title is not "Revelation" (or even "Revelations" as many people say) but "The Revelation of Jesus Christ"—or more accurately, "The Apocalypse of Jesus Christ". The words "apocalypse" and "apocalyptic" tend to mean, in modern English parlance, a terrible catastrophe, usually related to the end of the world or human civilization. Because of that common, modern, usage, we tend to think that's what the word actually means, but it isn't.

An "apocalypse" was a particular genre of literature in the 1st century BC to the 1st century AD. The word literally means an "unveiling". It doesn't mean to hide something in a cryptic way, nor does it necessarily have anything to do with the end of the world. It was a style; a genre of religious literature where historical events are described using the language of prophetic symbols, symbols which were very common to the people of that time, but which are not in common usage today. Such "apocalypses" appear in both Jewish and Christian writings from that period. For example, "The Apocalypse of Adam", "… of Baruch", "… of Paul", "... of Enoch", etc. In fact, the Book of Enoch was one of the most widely read apocalypses, and it is even quoted in the New Testament, when Jude quotes Enoch chapter 2:

Enoch, who lived in the seventh generation after Adam, prophesied about these people. He said, "Listen! The Lord is coming with countless thousands of his holy ones to execute judgment on the people of the world. He will convict every person of all the ungodly things they have done and for all the insults that ungodly sinners have spoken against him." Jude 14-15

So, with that in mind, the "Apocalypse of Jesus Christ" simply means **"an unveiling of the prophecy of Jesus Christ explained in the language of well-known prophetic symbols".**

What was the "prophecy" of Jesus Christ? It was the account we have just gone through in the last section—the Olivet discourse—the prophetic speech which Jesus gave to His disciples (Matthew 23-25). That was the only extended "prophecy" which Jesus gave. If we were to talk about "the Sermon of Jesus Christ," we would be talking about the Sermon on the Mount—His most extensive "sermon" (Matthew 5-7), and if we were to talk about the "Lord's Prayer", we would be referring to the model prayer He taught to His disciples (even though we know there are lots of other references of Him praying). Also, if we talk about the "Prophecy of Jesus Christ", we are obviously talking about the only extended prophecy that He delivered, and THAT prophecy was about what would happen within "one generation" (not OUR generation) when a time of trouble and tribulation would come to Judea (not to the whole word) which would begin when Jerusalem was surrounded by armies bearing the eagle banner (the Romans) and would end with the Temple being so obliterated that "not one stone will be left upon another".

THAT was what Jesus predicted and prophesied. THAT was the "End of the Age" and THAT would happen within forty years. If THAT was Jesus' prophecy, and if Revelation is an unveiling of Jesus' prophecy in the language of symbols, then THAT is what Revelation is about too. And it quite clearly is.

The Book of Revelation takes the only full prophecy that Jesus delivered, and amplifies it, gives greater detail, and explains it more fully, detailing not only what would soon occur in Judea (as Jesus did) but expanding it to what would happen in Asia Minor as well (as the book is addressed to churches in that region).

The beginning of Revelation—*"The revelation from Jesus Christ, which God gave him to show his servants* **what must soon take place.***"* (1:1)

The end of Revelation – *"Do not seal up the words of the prophecy of this book,* **for the time is near.***"* (22:10)

It's about prophecies that were about to be fulfilled, very soon, within the lifetime of the first readers. Revelation was, like Jesus' Olivet prophecy, also about events about to be fulfilled in the first century AD. And the structure of the book parallels Jesus Olivet prophecy exactly, but with some added detail and extra meat on the bones.

By now, the Jesus-movement has spread throughout the Roman Empire, and Asia Minor in particular (modern day Turkey) was being majorly impacted by this new faith. In fact, once Jerusalem was destroyed, the new faith would have no "centre" or "capital city" anymore—it would be spreading like a living yeast, leavening everything it came in contact with. There would be multiple centers of the faith—in Alexandria, Greece, Rome, even the British Isles received the message of the gospel within a few years of the resurrection of Christ, but of main importance next would be Asia Minor, because that is where so many new churches were being established, and that is where the next attacks on the new faith would come—both from within in the form of dualistic Gnosticism, and from without in the form of imperial persecution.

So, the book starts with John, who is imprisoned for his faith on the island of Patmos, (just off the coast of Asia Minor), writing seven letters to the seven major church centers in Asia Minor. While there is much symbolic (apocalyptic) language even in these "seven letters", these churches did exist, and he was writing to real people in real cities. Then, the vision goes into the heavenly realms, and John sees everything Jesus spoke of in His Olivet prophecy but he sees it in the language of symbols—the authorities of the Old Covenant system (the Jews) are joined by the pagan imperial powers (the Romans), and together, they persecute the new faith.

The structure of Revelation follows Jesus' Olivet prophecy very closely. Very soon, they would see the fulfillment of the first part of Jesus' prophecy—what was still a generation away when Jesus spoke it (around 30AD) was now only a few years away (around 64AD) and would "happen soon".

1. Within a few years, the Romans would invade Jerusalem and destroy the city and the Temple. There would also be persecution of the new faith throughout the Empire, especially in Asia Minor. Believers were to flee Jerusalem (called "Babylon" in Revelation) as the Romans would burn it to the ground. This is depicted as Jesus and heavenly armies riding on horseback in the sky over the city, and He has "a sharp two-edged sword in his mouth"—a creepy image if you take it literally, it means that the prophetic word in His mouth is now being fulfilled. (Revelation 4-19).

2. Then, there would be a long period of time when the gospel is going forth and believers in Christ are seated in heavenly thrones (which Ephesians 2:6-7 says is our current reality). This is the time we now live in, AFTER the tribulation of AD 66-70 but BEFORE the final return of Christ. During this time, "satan is bound" in a particular way, "that he may no longer deceive the nations". (Remember, Jesus came to "bind the strong man" Mark 3:11). The message of the gospel is going forth in all the world unhindered, and there is nothing the devil can do to stop it. This long period of time is figuratively given the number "1,000 years" because in Jewish symbolism, 1,000 = "everything"

(Psalm 50:10: the cattle on a thousand hills belongs to God—that means all cattle on all hills belong to God, etc.) (Revelation 20).

3. Then, there will be a final return of Christ, the final judgment, and the renewed creation (Revelation 21-22).

[For a full, verse-by-verse description of what each of Revelation's statements means and how they were fulfilled, see *The Days of Vengeance* by David Chilton]

CHAPTER 10:
APOCALYPTIC SYMBOLS

I can't do justice to this subject here, but I'll just give some examples of what apocalyptic symbols are and what they mean. Let's look at four symbols—The Woman with Child, The Two Beasts, The Harlot, and The New Creation from Revelation:

THE WOMAN WITH CHILD—REVELATION 12

Then a great and mysterious sign appeared in the sky. There was a woman, clothed in the sun and who had the moon under her feet and a crown of twelve stars on her head. She was soon to give birth, and the pains and suffering of childbirth made her cry out. Another mysterious sight appeared in the sky. There was a huge red dragon with seven heads and ten horns and a crown on each of his heads. With his tail he dragged a third of the stars out of the sky and threw them down to the earth. He stood in front of the woman, in order to eat her child as soon as it was born. Then she gave birth to a son, who will rule over all nations with an iron rod. But the child was snatched away and taken to God and his throne. The woman fled into the wilderness to a place prepared for her by God, where she might be taken care of for 1,260 days. (Revelation 12:1-6)

This is showing how a virgin girl from Israel would give birth to the Savior, and how the devil would work through one the political leaders at that time and would try to kill the Savior as a young child, but would fail, and eventually the Savior would return to God, while true Israel would flee from Jerusalem to be protected during the three and a half year war (1,260 days).

It is fascinating to note that this account in Revelation, as well as being an allegory, actually happened in the constellation of Virgo! The "woman clothed with the sun, with the moon beneath her feet, and a crown of 12 stars on her head" is quite clearly Virgo, but who does Virgo identify and signify? When we go back into the Old Testament, we see Joseph's dream of "the sun, moon, and eleven stars bowing down" to him (he himself, obviously being the 12th star).

The meaning of the dream is clear, as his father says to him, *"What is this dream you had? Will your mother and I and your brothers actually come and bow down to the ground before you?"* (Genesis 37:10). These people are the "patriarchs" of the future nation of Israel, each of the 12 sons being the founder of one of the 12 tribes of Israel, and they are symbolized as 12 stars (with the father & mother being the sun and moon). Using Old Testament symbolism, this woman is Israel! Or rather, she is a virgin mother from Israel – *"the Lord himself will give you the* **sign**. *Look! The virgin will conceive a child! She will give birth to a son and will call him Immanuel, which means 'God is with us'."* (Isaiah 7:14).

We don't know exact dates for Jesus conception and birth, but we know the general time period, and at that time, in the constellation of Virgo, the sun entered her "house" – Virgo became "pregnant" with the sun, and the moon was below her feet. Her young male child (Jesus) was threatened by "the dragon" (the constellation Draco) working through one of its "heads" (heads of state—Herod in this case, whose royal color was red) and had to flee. The son eventually "ascends" back to God in the image. Just before Jesus' ascension was His death and resurrection, and at the cross, there was an eclipse of the sun (Luke 23:45). We know from astronomy that an eclipse of the sun took place then, producing a "blood moon".

"Signs in the heavens above and wonders on the earth below, blood [*of Jesus on the cross] *fire* [*of the Holy Spirit at Pentecost] *and billows of smoke* [*at

the destruction of Jerusalem], *the sun shall be turned to darkness and the moon to blood red."* (Acts 2:17-19).

That blood moon eclipse took place once again in the constellation of Virgo, or to put that another way, when the bloody, dead body of Jesus was being taken down from the cross and laid at the feet of His mother, Mary, on earth; in the sky there was a blood moon lying at the feet of Virgo!

THE TWO BEASTS—IMPERIAL AND RELIGIOUS ROME—REVELATION 13

There are two great "Beasts" in the Book of Revelation—the Beast from the sea and the Beast from the land. The first Beast (from the sea) is a symbol of the Roman emperor. This Beast has 10 heads & crowns. These are the "heads of state" that ruled the region. The Beast specifically is identified with Nero. This Beast arises out of the (Mediterranean) sea, where the Roman Empire arose, and Nero was so hated by his own citizens that they referred to him as "that great beast". He recruited the pagan priests in the temples of Asia Minor to help him with his persecution of the Christians, (many of whom he had beheaded—the apostle Paul was beheaded by Nero).

What Nero (the Beast from the Sea) and his pagan priests of the Imperial cult (the Beast from the Land) did was to set up a system at the entrance to the Agora (marketplaces) in Asia Minor, with an idol of Nero as a god, and some burning incense in front of it, and only those who took the incense in their hand, wiped a mark of the ash on their forehead, and said "Nero is Lord" could enter to buy and sell. Nero's' name, in gematria (the ancient practice of using letters for numbers) adds up to 666 (Neron Kaiser—or Casear Nero).

Incidentally, it is well known by archeologists and historians that the Greek and Roman temple priests were experts at using mechanical means, special effects and ventriloquism to make statues look like they could cry, move, speak, and perform miracles. That is what we see in Revelation 13—not the anti-christ putting microchips under people's skin, but Nero beheading all who refused to worship the statues of the Emperor.

JERUSALEM THE HARLOT – REVELATION 17-19

Two cities are contrasted in Revelation—"Babylon" and the "New Jerusalem". The "New Jerusalem" is the Bride of Christ, the church (compare Revelation 21:2 with Hebrews 12:2, Galatians 4:26, and Ephesians 5:31-32). "Babylon" is the old Jerusalem—natural, physical, geographical Jerusalem. Jerusalem is referred to as a "harlot", echoing the words of the Old Covenant prophets who said the same thing— "the faithful city has become a harlot" (Isaiah 1:21).

Jerusalem is a harlot because she was once "married to the Lord", but she broke her covenant with God and "committed adultery" (see Rev 17:2 & 18:3 and Jeremiah 3:8) and she has rejected God's holy prophets and saints and even His Son, and killed them and will be held accountable for their blood:

*"I am sending you prophets and sages and teachers. Some of them you will kill and crucify; others you will flog in your synagogues and pursue from town to town. And so upon you will come all the righteous blood that has been shed on earth, from the blood of righteous Abel to the blood of Zechariah son of Berekiah, whom you murdered between the temple and the altar. Truly I tell you, all this will come upon **this generation**. Jerusalem, Jerusalem, you who kill the prophets and stone those sent to you, how often I have longed to gather your children together, as a hen gathers her chicks under her wings, and you were not willing. Look, your house is left to you desolate."* (Matthew 23:34-38)

"In her was found the blood of prophets and of God's holy people, of all who have been slaughtered on the earth." (Revelation 18:24)

As a "harlot" who was "under the Law", she would be stoned to death—the penalty for adultery:

"From the sky huge hailstones, each weighing about forty kilograms fell on people. And they cursed God on account of the plague of hail, because the plague was so terrible." (Revelation 16:21)

Josephus tells us in his history that when the Romans invaded Jerusalem, they used catapults with rocks and they painted them white (like hailstones) to make them harder to see in the daytime sky. Jerusalem, the "harlot" (the once faithful city, which has now rejected God and his ways and his prophets and his Son) is referred to as "Babylon", and as "Sodom" and as "Egypt"—all once great cities which became enemies of God and His people, who became sinful, and self-righteous, and violent, and wicked. Jerusalem is referred to as "Babylon—mother of harlots" who has been judged and will fall, and God's people are called to "come out of her, my people," and those who heeded Jesus' prophecy did flee from Jerusalem to the city of Pella before the Romans invaded, and by "coming out from her", they "endured to the end (of that Age) and they were saved". (See Rev 17-19).

So, Jerusalem is "the great city–which is figuratively called Sodom and Egypt—where also their Lord was crucified". (Rev. 11:8). The Temple in Jerusalem would be destroyed by the invasion of riders on horseback (see Rev. 14-15). And the final result would be that "Babylon" (Jerusalem) would be burned with fire and destroyed completely, ending the prominence of the city as a religious center and ensuring that the "New Jerusalem" would be a global community embracing all people everywhere through all the Ages:

"The smoke from that city ascends—till the end of the Age" (Rev 19:3)

Now, I am aware that some people teach that the "Harlot" is the United States, or the European Union, or the Vatican, or that it was ancient Rome, but it really doesn't work, and here is why:

- Rome (like the USA, the EU, etc.) was never "married" to God, so could not be accused of committing adultery against Him (but Israel was)

- Rome is never called a "harlot" elsewhere in the Bible, (but Israel is)

- Rome was never in a national covenant with God, so couldn't be judged for breaking that covenant, (but Israel was)

- Rome didn't have a central Temple which was destroyed; it had numerous pagan temples (but Jerusalem did).

- Rome and its emperors are pictured (as we shall see in a moment) as a great "Beast" upon whose back the "Harlot" gets a free ride for a period of time, then the "Beast" turns of the "Harlot" and devours her in the fire. How could Rome ride on the back of Rome and then turn on Rome and destroy Rome? And even if it could do those things, when did it happen? It's quite clear that Jerusalem is the "harlot" because Jerusalem was once the faithful city who had now become a harlot, had shed the blood of God's prophets and His Son, had leaders who were "sucking up" to Rome and were given power by Rome which they used to enrich themselves, was eventually turned on by Rome, invaded by Rome, "stoned" by Rome, and "devoured in fire" by Rome. The harlot is Jerusalem.

THE NEW CREATION—REVELATION 21

This is shown as a "new heaven, a new earth, and a new Jerusalem" (Rev 21). Spiritually speaking, figuratively and allegorically (remember that Revelation itself uses the word "symbolically" or "allegorically" in 11:8), this is a present reality. In Jewish parlance of the time, the city of Jerusalem symbolized "the earth" and the Temple in Jerusalem symbolized "the heavens" (with each of the three courts in the Temple symbolizing the "three heavens" – see 2 Corinthians 12:2).

The discipline of Sacred Geometry (practiced by many ancient cultures, not just the Hebrews) was used to demonstrate that a temple or religious structure was a kind of "mirror image" of "the heavens" (for example, in ancient Egypt, the Giza plateau was a mirror of heaven—the three pyramids symbolizing the three stars in Orion's belt; the sphinx symbolizing the constellation Leo, and the river Nile symbolizing the Milky Way). So, when the Temple and Jerusalem were destroyed in AD 70, in "theological jargon" that meant that the old "heaven & earth" had passed away, and all of its "elements" (the altar, menorah, all the Temple and sacrificial accoutrements) were destroyed in fire (2 Peter 3:10).

So, this is a current experience for those who are "awakened" or "reborn" or whose eyes have been "opened"—we dwell in a new heaven & earth; we are part of a New Jerusalem—a global community. We can drink freely of the spiritual living waters; we are His "bride", the "dwelling of God is with" us—here and now.

Yet, the picture also shows this image as the full and final end of all the Ages (all twelve "gates") and so, as more and more people "wake up" spiritually and open their eyes wide to see the living presence of God impregnating all things with His life and love, then the ultimate experience, at the full end of the Ages, is that what is now a "symbol" becomes a reality. That is, we will eventually "see" what we now "believe"—right now, "all things are beneath his (Christ's) feet", yet, it doesn't look like that yet, we don't "see" it yet—"In putting everything under his feet, God left nothing that is not subject to them. Yet, at present, we do not SEE everything subject to them." (Hebrews 2:8)

Revelation is such a big book, jam-packed with symbolic meaning, that there is no way I can deal with all the symbols here, but the ones I have shared so far should be enough to show you that: Revelation is about events which were to happen "soon" in the lifetime of the original readers; it concerns the end of the Old Covenant and the beginning of the New Covenant. It contains much astronomical language as well as Old Testament imagery because it deals with the Ages. It's not about nuclear wars and tsunamis in our lifetime; it is about the great transition of the Ages that took place in the first century AD.

If you have ever read anything by the great mythologist, Joseph Campbell or studied Carl Jung's theory of archetypes and the collective unconscious, then you are familiar with the power of mythic symbols. It seems that all human cultures have stories and myths which contain similar symbols and archetypes which all people in all cultures at all times seem to be able to see—both within their own psyches (as part of the human experience) or within the patterns that commonly reoccur in life. These archetypes and symbols and myths are present in scripture (a "myth" in the theological, cultural, or philosophical sense, does not mean "a story which is not true" but rather "a story which teaches truths") and Revelation uses symbols common in the apocalyptic genre (both Biblical and extra-Biblical) from the Old Testament, and from the constellations. It uses that language intentionally because it is the language of the unconscious mind, the spirit, the heart, the language that we dream in, and see visions.

Each picture certainly does paint a thousand words. By doing this, it shows (in picture language) what HAS happened in time and space in the destruction of the Old Covenant and the birth of the New, and also in a way which speaks timeless, universal truths that apply throughout all of history as well as in our individual lives, (theologically speaking, Revelation is "eschatological"—it speaks of the "end times" which were the end of that Age; it is "apocalyptic" in that it uses the genre of picture-symbols to communicate. It is "preterist" in that it is about events which are now in our past. It speaks of a now-past fulfillment, and it is "idealist" because its message rings through all the Ages and all life experiences with universal wisdom).

CHAPTER 11:
ASTRO-THEOLOGY

I mentioned that studying the Ages led to two Biblical mysteries—what the terms "Age", "End of the Age", and "Age-enduring" actually mean in the original languages and culture, and what the symbolic meaning of the zodiac (which features prominently in scripture) means. By living in a very different worldview, our eyes tend to be closed to these picture-symbols in scripture. But the more I studied, the more I discovered that it is only in recent times that we have lost these symbols and archetypes.

Archeologists have unearthed ancient synagogues in Israel with zodiac mosaics on their floors. Josephus said the Temple even had one, and for the last 2,000 years, Christians in the mainstream denominations have included the zodiac in their stain glass windows and carvings (usually connected to the Twelve Tribes of Israel and Twelve Apostles), and some even have old clocks that contain the zodiac as well as hours and minutes. Then there were the non-mainstream movements and denom-inations (like the Bogomils, Cathars, and Brethren of the Free Spirit) who taught about the Biblical and spiritual meaning of the Zodiac, especially emphasizing three Ages—the Age of the Father (Aries), the Age of the Son (Pisces), and the coming Age of the Spirit (Aquarius). We know that the early persecuted Christians in Rome hid in the catacombs, and there they painted Jesus as "the Great Fisherman of the Age of Pisces"! Where did they get these ideas? The Bible:

GENESIS 1:14

Then God said, "Let lights appear in the sky to separate the day from the night. Let them serve as **signs,** *and to mark the* **seasons,** *days, and years".*

The purpose of the sun and moon and stars are given as being a calendar—to mark days and years, and to be for **"signs"** and to mark **"seasons"**.

ACTS 2:19-20

"For there shall be signs in the heavens above, and wonders on the earth below".

The twelve signs of the zodiac mark something significant about specific periods of time. Avah, Hebrew for "signs", and Moed, Hebrew for "seasons," indicate that the stars mark something fixed or appointed—specifically prophetic and historical events. *As "signs",* as picture-symbols, the constellations contain a message—a message not in regular language or speech, but in the language of symbols:

THEY CONTAIN A MESSAGE: PSALM 19:1-4

The heavens declare the glory of God. The skies display his craftsmanship. Day after day they continue to speak; night after night they make him known. They speak without a sound or word; their voice is never heard. Yet their message has gone throughout the earth, and their words to all the world.

THEIR MESSAGE IS THE GOSPEL: ROMANS 10:17-18

Paul quotes the above verse about the message of the stars, and says they have proclaimed the "gospel" in their message:

So faith comes from hearing, that is, hearing the Gospel about Christ. But I ask, have the people of Israel actually heard the message? Yes, they have: "their message has gone throughout the earth, and their words to all the world." (Romans 10:17-18)

THEIR MESSAGE MARKS TIME PERIODS: GENESIS 1:14

Then God said, "Let lights appear in the sky to separate the day from the night. Let them serve as signs, and mark the seasons, days, and years".

We will come back to these time periods. First, let's look at the constellations as "signs". What is the message each picture-symbol contains? This part of the zodiac is much more well known, and many books have been written about it from Lutheran, Reformed, Evangelical, and Pentecostal traditions. The original meaning of the zodiac was a message written out in 12 word-pictures that tell a story—the story in the sky, the message in the heavens, the gospel in the stars. We will deal very briefly with their annual message (there is a list of books for further study on this topic at the end of this book).

The zodiac is a cycle of 12 constellations—with a different one prominent each month, all 12 signs making up the 12 months of the year (our Western calendars have been changed and each constellation now goes from halfway through one month to halfway through the next month. But in ancient calendars, each month was aligned to one constellation). So, throughout the course of a year, the full message was "proclaimed" silently by the heavens above (which the ancients were more familiar with than us due to a lack of light pollution and the fact that they didn't really have very much else to look at during dark nights, except the sky).

But because they are in a cycle, where do we start and end? Even though the zodiac is a repeating cycle, we know that Virgo is the place to start because the earliest ancient zodiac that we have is in the Egyptian temple at Dendera, where we see a painting of the circle of the zodiac, but it is broken by the Sphinx (a "living creature" like we see in Scripture) whose human face is pointing towards Virgo, and whose lion body is pointing towards Leo. So, the circle starts with Virgo and ends with Leo (it's worth remembering that Moses was "schooled in all the wisdom of Egypt" – Acts 7:22).

"The first Bible was in the sky, called the zodiac…And notice, in the zodiac, what did it start off with? The first thing in the zodiac is the Virgin. The last thing in the zodiac is Leo the lion. The first coming of Christ, through the virgin. The Second Coming, Leo the lion, the Lion of the tribe of Judah." **William Branham. (1909-1965)**

Here is a very brief description of their message as "signs" (there are many books, both ancient and modern, which explain in detail the story of the stars, and it is a subject which is once again gaining prominence. In this book, we are more interested in the "seasons" which they mark). Each constellation also has "Decans" or smaller constellations which accompany them. These are less known, but I will include them as they make the meaning of each constellation clear:

1. VIRGO THE VIRGIN

The virgin will give birth to a Son.

Depicted as a woman with a bundle of wheat in one hand and a branch in the other. The brightest star is in the seed of the wheat (Spica—"the branch"). This is a prophecy of the coming of "the Branch" ("Here is the man whose name is the Branch, and he will branch out from his place and build the temple of the Lord". Zechariah 6:12, "In that day, the Branch of the Lord will be beautiful and glorious" Isaiah 4:2)—the promised Savior who comes from a Virgin. ("The virgin will conceive and give birth to a son, and will call him Immanuel." Isaiah 7:14).

Decans:

1) Coma—"the desired one". ("the desire of all nations shall come" Haggai 2:7). Depicted as a virgin with a newborn baby on her lap.

2) Bootes—"the coming one". Depicted as a harvester with a sickle. ("I looked, and there before me was a white cloud, and seated on the cloud was one like a son of man with a crown of gold on his head and a sharp sickle in his hand." Revelation 14:14).

3) Centaurus—"two natures". Depicted as half man, half horse. It represents the physical and spiritual nature of Jesus. ("God was manifest in the flesh" 1 Timothy 3:16).

2. LIBRA THE SCALES

This savior will pay for our debt of sin and balance the scales of justice

Depicted as scales representing justice and the condition of man. ("You have been weighed in the balances and found wanting."—Daniel 5:27). On one side of the balance is the star Zuben Al Chemali—"the price which covers" indicating the sufficient price paid by the seed of the Virgin (Jesus). ("Then I looked and saw a black horse, and its rider held in his hand a pair of scales." Revelation 6:5).

Decans:

1) Crux—The Southern Cross. The sufficient payment was by way of the Cross.

2) Lupus—(in Latin Victima—"the victim"). The Savior was a victim for our sins, not His own.

3) Corona Borealis—"the northern crown". The Son of the Virgin became a victim on the Cross so that He could attain the heavenly crown.

3. SCORPIO THE SCORPION

Evil will sting the Savior but will itself be crushed by Him

Depicted as a scorpion. In Coptic, it means "the attack of the enemy". In early cultures, this constellation was pictured as a dragon or a serpent (Revelation 20:2). ("And I will put enmity between you and the woman, and between your offspring and hers; he will crush your head, and you will strike his heel." Genesis 3:15. "I have given you authority to trample on snakes and scorpions and to overcome all the power of the enemy; nothing will harm you." Luke 10:19).

Decans:

1) The Serpent (or Serpens). Depicted trying to grab the Northern Crown, but is restrained by Ophiuchus. The North represents Heaven.

2) Ophiuchus—Depicted with his heel being attacked by Scorpio, while he is bruising the head of The Serpent (Genesis 3:15).

3) Hercules—Depicted as beating a snake in the branches of a tree (the Tree of Knowledge of Good and Evil).

4. SAGITTARIUS THE ARCHER

Where we have missed the mark and fallen short,
He will come down to earth and point us to the heavens

Depicted as a centaur, indicating the two natures of Jesus (spiritual and physical), with a bow and arrow aimed at the heart of Scorpio. Jesus will be victorious over Satan. ("I looked, and behold, a white horse! And its rider had a bow, and a crown was given to him, and he came out conquering, and to conquer." Revelation 6:2, "For everyone has sinned {missed the target} we all fall short of God's glorious standard." Romans 3:23).

Decans:

1) Lyra—Depicted as a harp (indicating praise). The brightest star in Lyra is Vega—"he shall be exalted".

2) Ara—"It is finished". Depicted as an altar upside down, with its fire pouring over the South Pole, or "the regions of darkness". It represents no more sacrifice for sin.

3) Draco—"the dragon". Four-thousand, seven-hundred years ago, Thuban, the brightest star, was the Polar star. Through astronomical precession, Polaris is now the Polar star. Thuban has been displaced or "kicked out" of its heavenly position, like Satan (Revelation 12:9).

5. CAPRICORN THE FISH-GOAT

The scapegoat of atonement slain for the redeemed.

Depicted as a goat with the tail of a fish. There are two stars in the head: Deneb Algedi—"the sacrifice comes" and Dabih—"the sacrifice slain". In Old Testament times, the sins of the people were placed on a goat called the scapegoat, (Leviticus 9:15-17, 10:16-17) just as Jesus bears our sin. A fish has been the symbol of Christianity for 2000 years (see Jeremiah 16:15, Ezekiel 47:1-9). Both the goat and the fish remind us of the sacrifice of Jesus.

Decans:

1) Sagitta—"The arrow of God's judgment"

2) Aquila—"The falling eagle". The brightest star Al Okal—"wounded in the heel". (Gen. 3:15)

3) Delphinus—"dolphin"—a creature born of water.

6. AQUARIUS THE WATER BEARER

The living waters of the Spirit being poured out on all people.

Jesus said whoever drank the water He offered would never thirst. His water "shall be in him a well of water springing up into everlasting life" (John 4:14). Living water is a symbol of the Holy Spirit, who was poured out on Pentecost. "The water bearer". "Whosoever drinks of my water shall never thirst"; John 4:14.

Decans:

1) Pisces Australis—"The southern fish". Aquarius is depicted pouring water (the spirit) on the fish, symbolizing the Church.

2) Cygnus—"The swan of the Northern Cross". The constellation is a swan, but the stars form a cross.

3) Pegasus—depicted as a winged, white horse. The brightest star is Markab—"returning from afar". Pegasus reminds us of Jesus' "coming" in the fulfillment of His prophecy in Revelation 19.

7. Pisces The Fish

The multitudes who will follow the Savior, who is the great fisher of men.

Depicted as two fish and has been the symbol of Christianity for 2000 years. In the First Century, the Greek word "ichthus" (Greek for "fish") became the symbol for Christianity, and early Christians were publicly referred to as Ichthus and Pisces. Jesus' ministry began with a great catch of fish, and He told His followers, "I will make you fishers of men". In the Gospel of Matthew, the fish is used as a symbol for the kingdom of heaven (Matt. 4:19, 13:47-50). In Coptic, (Picot Orion), "congregation," or "company of the coming Prince." The Two Fishes multiply into generations of believers as the gospel spreads.

Decans:

1) The Band—a band which binds the two fish together (with unbreakable chords).

2) Andromeda—"the assembly". Depicted as a chained woman (the Bride of Christ who was once bound by sin).

3) Cepheus—"the royal branch, the king". Depicted as a king with a robe and crown. Two of the stars in this constellation are: Al Phirk—"the redeemer", Al Rai—"the shepherd". This must be King Jesus, our shepherd and redeemer.

8. Aries The Ram or Lamb

The wounded and slain sacrifice, who takes away our sins.

Depicted as a ram. The brightest star is Elnath—"the wounded or slain". This is a symbol of the sacrificial system, which began when the Lord Himself provided Abraham with a ram as a sacrificial offering, and it continued throughout the Old Covenant until Jesus came as the final sacrifice.

Decans:

1) Cassiopeia—Depicted as a woman sitting on a throne, fixing her hair and adjusting her robes, preparing herself for the king ("the time has come for the wedding feast of the Lamb, and his bride has prepared herself" Revelation 19:7).

2) Perseus—"the breaker". Depicted as a soldier with a helmet and sword. In his left hand is the head of Medusa-"trodden under foot". The principal star in the head of Medusa is Al Ghoul—"the evil spirit". Also, there is Rosh Satan—"the head of Satan". Medusa's hair is snakes.

3) Cetus—Depicted as a sea monster in the southern sky (representative of Hell). The star in the neck is Mira—"the rebel". The brightest star is Menkar—"the bound or chained enemy".

(*"I saw an angel coming down out of heaven, having the key to the Abyss and holding in his hand a great chain. He seized the dragon, that ancient serpent, who is the devil, or Satan, and bound him for a thousand years. He threw him into the Abyss, and locked and sealed it over him"* Revelation 20:1-3)

9. TAURUS THE BULL

The Coming One will push forth like a bull or ox, and plough the field of the world, bringing forth a harvest.

Depicted as a raging, charging bull. Only the front half is depicted. Where the back should be, is Aries, as if the bull is coming out of Aries. A wild bull was the symbol of power and rule. Taurus means governor, captain or leader. On the shoulder of Taurus are the Pleiades—"the congregation of the judge". ("Can you bind the chains of the Pleiades?

Can you loosen Orion's belt? Can you bring forth the constellations in their seasons" Job 38:31)

Decans:

1) Auriga—Depicted as the great shepherd holding a she-goat and kids in his lap. In the centre of the goat is Capella—"she-goat". In the foot of the shepherd is Elnath—"the wounded". Our shepherd, Jesus, was wounded in the heel.

2) Orion—"coming forth as light". The brightest star is Betelgeuse—"the coming of the branch". Jesus is the Branch. In Orion's foot is Rigel—"the foot that crushes". In the shoulder is Bellatrix—"quickly coming". In the leg is Saiph—"bruised". Again, our shepherd was wounded (symbolically) in the heel.

3) Eridanus—"river of fire". This constellation runs across the heavens toward the south. In the river are Archernar—"the afterpart of the river", Cursa—"bent down" and Zourac—"flowing". ("He sat on a fiery throne with wheels of blazing fire, and a river of fire was pouring out, flowing from his presence." Daniel 7:9)

10. GEMINI THE TWINS

The one with Twin-natures will come as the repairer of the first couple's transgression.

In the ancient zodiac, Gemini are not only Twins, but one is male and one female. As it was in the beginning, so it shall be in the end. The Bible starts with a couple in the Garden of Eden (Adam & Eve), and it ends with Jesus the Groom and the church His Bride at the end of the Bible. In Coptic, Gemini is Pimahi—"the united". Two stars mark the two heads, Castor and Pollux. Castor—"ruler" or "judge"; Pollux—"wounded, hurt, afflicted". ("After three months, we put out to sea in a ship that had wintered in the island—it was an Alexandrian ship with the figurehead of the twins Castor and Pollux." Acts 28:11)

Decans:

1) Canis Major—The major star in this constellation is Sirius, the brightest star in the sky—"the prince".

2) Canis Minor—the brightest star is Procyon—"redeemer". The Egyptians called it Sebak—"the conquering" or "victorious".

3) Lepus—originally, a snake. It is located under the feet of Orion, who crushes the head of Lepus, the snake. The brightest star is Arneb—"the enemy of him who comes". Also, Nihal—"the mad", and Sulya—"the deceiver". Satan is the enemy of Jesus and is the deceiver (Genesis 3:13).

11. CANCER THE CRAB

The multitude of the redeemed, gathered together in the Good Shepherd's sheepfold.

Depicted as a crab (born of water)—"to hold or encircle". In some ancient Zodiacs, Cancer was known as the cattlefold or the sheepfold. The brightest star is Tegmine—"holding". Also, Acubene—"sheltering or hiding place"; Ma'Alaph—"assembled thousands"; and Al Himarean—"kids or lambs". It also contains a cluster of stars called Praesepe—"multitude". ("After this I looked, and there before me was a great multitude that no one could count, from every nation, tribe, people and language, standing before the throne and before the Lamb." Revelation 7:9)

Decans:

1) Ursa Minor—the Little Dipper. In ancient times, it was depicted as a sheepfold. Ursa Minor has seven bright stars and twenty-four in the

entire constellation (the seven bright lamps before the Throne of God and the twenty-four elders who serve Him—Revelation 1:13 and 4:4).

2) Ursa Major—"the Big Dipper" (in North America) or "the Plough" (in the UK). Originally "the assembled flock". The brightest star is Dubeh—"a herd or flock"; Merach—"the flock purchased"; Phaeda—"visited, guarded or numbered"; and Benet Naish—"daughters of the assembly". (See John 10).

3) Argo—a ship. The image of Jesus and His disciples on a fishing boat has always been a symbol of Christ with His missional church.

12. LEO THE LION

He will return at the end of the Ages, as the lion of Judah

Leo is depicted as jumping on Hydra. This constellation shows the final battle and is the last celestial sign. As noted earlier, the Sphinx has a head of a woman (Virgo) and the body of a lion (Leo). Revelation describes Jesus as the "Lion of the Tribe of Judah". First, He came as a lamb. His Second Coming will be as a lion. "The lion of the tribe of Judah has prevailed" (Revelation 5:5). "The last enemy that will be abolished is death." (1 Corinthians 15:26)

Decans:

1) Hydra—"he who is abhorred". Depicted as a giant serpent extending about one-third of the circumference of the heavens. (Satan, the great dragon, took one—third of the stars with him—Revelation 12:4.)

2) Crater—a cup or bowl (see Revelation 16). This constellation is composed of thirteen stars.

3) Corvus—depicted as a bird eating the flesh of Hydra. (Revelation 19:17-19).

The entire panorama of the stars and their ancient names display the coming Savior. That's the story they tell every year. Each year contains twelve chapters to a story that God wrote in the sky, and that story is about the Savior who came and died and rose again. Even before humans had written language, they had the Bible in the sky.

Let's look at them as markers of "seasons" now—as the ancient calendar of the Ages....

CHAPTER 12:
THE CALENDAR OF THE AGES

Not only does each zodiac sign last for a month, each one also lasts for an Age—the Great Year has 12 Ages with each Age connected to one constellation, just like the year has twelve months, each connected to one constellation.

The stars and constellations appear to rotate around the Earth slowly. This is caused by the earth's own rotation within the greater rotation of the universe. Like a wobbling top, the orientation of the Earth's axis is slowly but continuously changing as it traces out a conical shape over a 25,625-year cycle. About every 2,160 years, the sun moves into another new zodiacal constellation, and each Age is a progressive step upwards for humanity, as we gradually lay aside childish things, and go on to maturity, becoming more and more spiritually enlightened, wise, and civilized.

This was known as the Great Year in the ancient world—the regular year having 12 months, the Great Year having 12 Ages. Each of these 12 constellations marks a particular period of time—an "Age". Most ancient cultures had Ages as part of their calendar. Plato used it, the Hindu Yugas have their Ages, even the Mayan calendar showed the "end of an Age" in 2012 (which was popularly, but incorrectly, proclaimed to be "the end of the world"—there we go, misunderstanding the end of an Age for the end of the world again).

It is important to say a word about the dates I have put for when an Age begins and ends. It doesn't really work as clearly as I have put it. If you do some research, you will see that different people move the dates backwards or forwards by a few decades. That is because each Age "descends" for a period of time while the next Age is "ascending"— with both Ages visible together for a Transition Period. Do you say that an Age has ended when the next Age begins to ascend, or when the first Age has fully disappeared? The dates I have put are approximate but also have the highest consensus. Perhaps this is a good place to point out that I am not talking about horoscopes or fortune telling, (that is what the Babylonians did with the constellations), but rather, the constellations serve two main purposes—to mark seasons and to be signs—to mark out time periods (Ages) and to tell a message (the gospel or good news).

As a cycle, after all the twelve ages have transpired (just over 25,000 years), they just start again in cyclical form. I don't know for sure how long the planet has been here, and how long the constellations have painted their story on our sky, or how many Ages transpired before the ones I will mention, so I will only mention five that synchronize with the Biblical narrative, and two in particular (Aries and Pisces—the Old Covenant and the arrival of the New Covenant):

AGE OF GEMINI THE TWINS— 6450 BC TO 4300 BC—THE AGE OF DUALITY

Biblically, this is the time of Adam and Eve. The Gemini twins are often depicted as a man and a woman holding hands. In the Biblical story, because of their desire for "the knowledge of good and evil", they lost their paradise-like experience. The "Knowledge of Good and Evil" is dualism. Before that, they didn't know good and bad, right and wrong; they only knew The Tree of Life. Now, they brought sin and dualistic thinking into their world, which brought a sense of separation between the creation and Creator, humanity and God, male and female, Cain and Abel, and so on.

THE AGE OF TAURUS THE BULL— 4300 BC TO 2150 BC—THE AGE OF AGRICULTURE

The ancient people worshipped a number of bull deities during this time. In Egypt, they had Apis; the Greeks had Poseidon, the Bull of the Sea and his offspring, the Minotaur, as well as Zeus, the Bull-ravisher of Europa who fled over the Taurus mountains. Bull worshiping cults began to form in Assyria, Egypt, and Crete. Paganism and idolatry were widespread.

AGE OF ARIES THE RAM—2150 BC TO 70 AD— THE AGE OF SACRIFICE AND LAW CODES

The sacrifice of Abraham's ram occurred at the beginning of the Age of Aries. The ancient world contained a lot of human and child sacrifices to demonic-like gods and goddesses. So, when God spoke to Abraham and told him to offer his son, Isaac, as a sacrifice, Abraham doesn't even flinch, he just gets on with it. That is shocking to us because we don't understand their culture and how "normal" that kind of idea was. But God didn't actually want him to sacrifice his son. God was against human sacrifice and was about to give humanity an "upgrade" away from that kind of barbaric thinking.

When Isaac asks his father where the sacrifice is, Abraham answers, "The Lord Himself will provide a lamb". The story continues, "When they reached the place God had told him about, Abraham built an altar there and arranged the wood on it. He bound his son Isaac and laid him on the altar, on top of the wood. Then he reached out his hand and took the knife to slay his son. But the angel of the Lord called out to him from heaven, "Abraham! Abraham!" "Here I am," he replied. "Do not lay a hand on the boy," he said. "Do not do anything to him. Now I know that you fear God, because you have not withheld from me your son, your only son." Abraham looked up and there in a thicket he saw a ram caught by its horns. He went over and took the ram and sacrificed it as a burnt offering instead of his son." (Genesis 22:8-13). This was the start of the Age of Aires, the Ram, the Age of the sacrificial system and eventually (under Moses) the Law code.

The Age of Aries was an Age of incredible change. Archetypally, Aries has to do with the development of identity, the "I am" that each of us carries within. It was during this Age that God reveals Himself as "I AM" (Exodus 3:14). Out of this understanding, monotheism was born, not just amongst the Hebrews but amongst other ancient people (For example, Pharaoh Akhenaten, who overthrew the Egyptians gods and replaced them with one God who was symbolized by the sun, was born around 1351BC). Around the globe, law codes were created—the Code of Hammurabi, the Twelve Tablets of Roman Law, the Edicts of Solon, the Analects of Confucius, along with the teachings of Lao Tzu, Socrates, Plato, and Aristotle. But Biblically speaking, the great Law Code event was The Ten Commandments and the Law of Moses.

During this time period, the Ram became a religious symbol in many places, replacing the former image of the Bull (Taurus). That is what the whole Golden Calf incident in Exodus 32 was about. Just as Moses is up the mountain getting the Ten Commandments which would be the foundation of the Old Covenant Law, the people are at the foot of the mountain making a golden calf—the symbol of the previous Age—the Age of Taurus. People have a strange attachment to previous Ages and have a fear of letting them go and venturing out into the unfamiliar new Age. Today, we see many Christians trying to hold on to the Old Covenant Laws and promises, and developing theologies and forms of worship that attempt to resurrect the Age of Aries (some even going so far as to wish for a new Temple to be built in Jerusalem and a sacrificial system restored—something which the whole Book of Hebrews warns against as apostasy from faith in Christ).

In the story of the Exodus, we see the Israelites trying to revive a theology and worship from the previous Age of Taurus. During the Age of Taurus, there were lots of "bull" religions—many of which died out as the Age of Aires progressed, but some which hung around, and so there were religions which killed bulls as a sign of killing off the old, previous Age (for example, in the mystery religion of Mithras, a bull is killed as a symbol of that very act).

Moses, in condemning the worship of the golden calf (Taurus), symbolically declared a new age had begun. Moses also gave instructions in the building of the tabernacle made of ram's skin.

Aries began to descend around 6 BC (and Pisces began to ascend). Remember that there are crossover times when both signs are visible—one descending and another ascending—these "transition periods" last for many decades. Aries started to descend at the time Jesus was conceived, and Pisces started to ascend, but Aries didn't fully "pass away" until 70 AD. This is called in astronomy **The Cusp of the Ages**, and in Theology as a **Transition Period.** We will look at that shortly.

THE AGE OF PISCES THE FISH—6 BC TO 2150 AD— THE CURRENT AGE NOW BEGINNING TO DESCEND.

The early Christians were persecuted by both the Jews and the Romans. They needed to come up with a way to protect themselves, so they started to meet in secret during times of persecution. But what about people who wanted to join them? They needed to know the secret symbol—the fish. I'm sure you have seen Christians who have the fish symbol on their car. It comes from the Greek word for fish—Icthus—which the early Christians used as an anagram for Jesus Christ, God's Son, Saviour (Iēsous Christos, Theou Yios, Sōtēr). But why did they pick a fish? Because they knew it was the start of the Age of Pisces, and Jesus had ushered that Age in. As previously mentioned, in the catacombs of Rome, Christians had painted a depiction of Jesus as "The Great Fisherman of the Age of Pisces". They understood the Age.

Pisces is two fish swimming in opposite directions, yet fused together in union, such that they cannot be released from each other. It symbolizes the coming together of the mind and the heart as well as the merging of the East and West, (Hebraic and Greek worldviews) something that is still in process. The fact that the two fish are swimming in opposite directions is interesting. It seems that the last 2,000 years have been pretty dualistic and Christianity has been a big part of that. Some people want to get rid of all religion and rush into the spiritual freedom of Aquarius, while others are trying to pull us back to Old Covenant observation and Aries-like religion.

Jesus' ministry started in the waters of baptism and ended with Him commissioning His disciples to go throughout the world and baptizing others (see Matthew 3 and 28). To quote Tertullian (155-240 AD), "Christians are little fish who are born in the waters of baptism". Jesus ministry began with a miraculous catch of fish, and it also ended with one (see Luke 5 and John 21). I see this as the great ingathering of people in the first century, and again in our own century.

THE AGE OF AQUARIUS—HAS ALREADY BEGUN TO ASCEND, AND WILL BE SOLE SIGN BY 2150 AD

The New Covenant continues on through this Age (and all Ages to Come—Ephesians 2:7) as the Kingdom of God continues to expand and grow. This will be an Age of increased "spirituality" and a decrease in "religion". I think there will be major shifts for the church and its style, structure, and ethos. It is a time when the outpouring of the Holy Spirit in fullness will be experienced all over the world, as God's Spirit continues to be poured out on all flesh (Acts 2:17), when all people will know the Lord (Jeremiah 31:34), and God's glory shall cover the earth as the waters cover the sea (Habakkuk 2:14). Good days are ahead!

THE CUSP OF THE AGES: THE TRANSITION PERIOD WHEN THE OLD COVENANT WAS DESCENDING, WHILE THE NEW COVENANT WAS ASCENDING— AD 30-70.

The "Old Covenant" Age was the Age of preparation—when God was preparing a people through whom He would send the Messiah to be the Savior of the world. It was going to take a whole Age to prepare the world for the arrival of Jesus. That Age was the Age of Aires—the Age of the Ram; the Age of the Sacrificial System and Law Code. It started with Abraham discovering that "the Lord himself will provide a ram" (Genesis 22:8), and it ended with Jesus as the final "scapegoat", the "Lamb of God who takes away the sin of the world" (John 1:29).

The Age of Aires started around 2160 BC, (give or take a number of decades due to the time it takes for an "ascent" and "descent" of an Age). Abraham is dated to approximately the same period, according to Biblical chronology. So, the Old Covenant Age (of Aries) started with the sacrifice of the ram which God provided, continued through the Mosaic Law and history of Old Testament Israel and their Temple cult and sacrificial system, and ended with the 'full and final sacrifice'—the death of Jesus Himself.

GENESIS 22:13

"Abraham looked up and there in a thicket he saw a ram caught by its horns. He went over and took the ram and sacrificed it as a burnt offering instead of his son."

Now, in the story, we read something crucial, but lost to most of us—God was establishing this "covenant" which included the provision of a "promised land" for the duration of that Age. God didn't promise the land to Abraham and his descendants as an "everlasting possession" but as an "Age-enduring possession". As mentioned, some of our English translations of the Bible often mistranslate that promise, which causes all sorts of confusion today. However, once we discover that the word is NOT "everlasting" but rather, "age-enduring", this completely undermines the apocalyptic preaching that is common which suggests that what is happening in the Middle East today is some kind of fulfillment of Bible prophecy. That prophecy was fulfilled almost 2,000 years ago, and that Age came to an end, and the promise was then fulfilled and God's original purpose of embracing all people, all cultures, all ethnic groups became clear. "God is no respecter of persons because he accepts people of all nations." (Acts 10:34-35). And it was fulfilled by the land being promised for an Age, inhabited for an Age, and then that Age coming to an end.

Here it is in Young's Literal Translation – *"And I have established My covenant between Me and thee, and thy seed after thee, to their generations, for **a covenant age-enduring**, to become God to thee, and to thy seed after thee."*

That Promised Land was to be in Abraham's descendant's possession for the entirety of the Age of Aries. That's why it started with the Ram which the Lord provided, and ended with the death of Jesus at Passover, (the "lamb of God who takes away the sin of the world"), when the Old Covenant was made "obsolete" and fully "passed away" within one generation during "the Last Days" at the "end of the Age" when the Temple and the totality of the sacrificial system was destroyed by the Romans in AD 70, in fulfillment of Jesus' prophecy—no Temple, no sacrificial system, no Age of Aries.

HEBREWS 8:13

"When God speaks of a "new" covenant, it means he has made the first one obsolete. It is now out of date and will soon disappear."

MATTHEW 24:1-3

"Jesus left the temple and was walking away when his disciples came up to him to call his attention to its buildings. "Do you see all these things?" he asked. "Truly I tell you, not one stone here will be left on another; every one will be thrown down." As Jesus was sitting on the Mount of Olives, the disciples came to him privately. "Tell us," they said, "when will this happen, and what will be the sign of your presence and of the end of the Age?"

So, the Old Covenant Age, (the Sacrificial Age, the Age of Aries), promised Israel a covenant with God and a promised land for the entirety of that Age—from Abraham through to Moses, through to the Temple of Solomon, through to the Exile in Babylon and the return to rebuild the Temple (Ezra and Nehemiah) until the time of Jesus and the final destruction of the Temple in AD 70 in fulfillment of Jesus' prophecy. That Age was then over, gone, disappeared, wiped out, served its purpose, fulfilled. To quote Jesus, "It is finished!"

THE NEW COVENANT

Throughout this Old Covenant Age, all along, God was promising people that this was only a temporary covenant; it was only for an Age. It would be superseded by a new covenant, and that covenant would begin with the people He had prepared—the descendants of Abraham, but it wouldn't be confined to them—no, as Peter said:

- *"Now, I really understand that God doesn't show favoritism rather, whoever respects God and does what is right is acceptable to him in any nation."* (Acts 10:34-35).

- *"The earth is the Lord's and everything in it, the world and all that it contains"* (Psalm 24:1).

- *"The earth will be filled with the knowledge of the glory of the Lord as the waters cover the sea"* (Habakkuk 2:14).

God loves and cares for all people, and welcomes all people into His kingdom—His new world which is emerging amongst us, and His new way of living. But this covenant would be offered first of all to the people who were prepared for the coming of this new and living way throughout the period of the Old Covenant:

JEREMIAH 31:32-34:

The days are coming,' declares the Lord, 'when I will make a new covenant with the people of Israel and with the people of Judah. It will not be like the covenant I made with their ancestors when I took them by the hand to lead them out of Egypt, because they broke my covenant, though I was a husband to them,' declares the Lord. This is the covenant that I will make with the people of Israel after that time,' declares the Lord. 'I will put my law in their minds and write it on their hearts. I will be their God, and they will be my people. No longer will they teach their neighbor, or say to one another, "Know the Lord," because they will all know me, from the least of them to the greatest,' declares the Lord. 'For I will forgive their wickedness and will remember their sins no more.'

CHAPTER 13:
WHAT STILL LIES AHEAD?

If the New Covenant is here to stay, and the Kingdom of God will continue to advance and increase, what does the next Age, the Age of Aquarius hold for us, and how will it be different? And do the 12 Ages continue to run on a perpetual cycle, or do they eventually come to an end?

The last 2,000+ years have been the New Covenant Age or Age of Pisces. To be honest, the term "New Covenant Age" is the wrong way to put it because although the Old Covenant came to an end in 70 AD, the New Covenant continues on forever, even though this Age will come to an end. The New Covenant lasts forever because it is mediated by Jesus, who lives forever (Hebrews 7:25). But certainly, the current Age, (the Age of Pisces) does come to an end, and the New Covenant continues on in expanded growth into the next Age, because the New Covenant ushered in the "Kingdom of God" or "the reign of God" or, as one translation puts it, "God's New World and New Way of Living", (The Good as New translation of the New Testament).

God is progressively creating this new world and a new way of living, and He is doing it through people. As people change, as people embrace God's new world and new way of living, and come into greater and greater harmony with how things are truly supposed to be, so they become a positive influence upon their world, and like a small piece of yeast put into some dough, it gradually spreads with a life of its own and "leavens the whole batch" (Luke 13:21) or like a tiny seed planted in the ground, it gradually grows and becomes a fruitful tree and provides shelter for others, (Matthew 13:31-33). Just as the Universe continues to expand at the speed of light, so God's Kingdom continues to expand as His light shines forth more and more in and through the lives, beliefs, behavior, and influence of more and more people. We are collaborators in creation.

ISAIAH 9:7

Of the increase of his government and of peace there will be no end

So, the Age of Pisces will end, the Age which began with, and will culminate in a miraculous catch of "fish". We are living in a time when the Age of Pisces is descending and the Age of Aquarius is dawning. I have already pointed out that Ages overlap for quite some period of time and it is difficult to put an exact time on when one Age has started and when the previous Age has finally, fully passed away, but by circa 2150AD, the Age of Pisces will have fully passed away, and the Age of Aquarius will be the only ruling Age. However, Pisces is already "descending", and Aquarius is already "ascending"—changes are underway.

So, what does this next Age look like? As God's kingdom continues to advance, and as many people are being influenced by God's new world which is emerging in our midst and His new way of living revealed in and through Jesus, what does it blossom into? There is much talk about the coming Aquarian Age both inside the Christian church, and outside of it in alternative spiritualities, in other religions, even in the secular world. Everyone has their own take on what the coming Age looks like, and to be honest, some of those ideas have very little to do with Jesus, the scriptures, or the true nature of God. Some ideas are positively occult and superstitious. I'm not talking about those kinds of ideas. I don't see the coming Age as one where the streets will be full of occult bookshops and crystal ball gazers, all claiming to be part of the Aquarian Age.

I see the coming Age as one where all superstition, (including religious traditions which make the true message that Jesus brought of no effect – Mark 7:13) is laid aside and where people start to let God's new way of living truly work in their lives—transforming, growing spiritually, becoming the people they were created to be—fully alive, fully loving, fully 'human', fully living out their true nature as image bearers of God, living by the meaning and spirit of the message of Jesus, and in so doing, changing the way they relate to the world around them so that this "new way of living" truly promotes the emergence of a "new world".

Imagine a world where it is commonplace, almost normal and taken for granted for people to have faith in an unconditionally loving, present Papa God, follow the teachings of Jesus regarding loving God and loving others. A world where people thrive in every way—physically, mentally, and spiritually, discover their gifts, talents and abilities and earn their living and live their lives doing the things which make them come alive. A world where violence is seen as a primitive horror from the past, and where God is honored, Jesus is followed, and people are loved and blessed in multiple ways. Likewise where businesses and politics and economics are run honestly and ethically, where ecology is valued, and where the Sermon on the Mount is lived out.

None of this is done by force, or by law, or certainly not by violence and war—it's not one religion or one culture forcing itself on others and seeking to stamp all others out. Rather, it is one presence (God) gradually changing lives and working in and through ALL cultures and people.

It is fascinating to notice that the Decans or "heralds" of Aquarius began to appear around the time of the Azusa Street revival and the birth of Pentecostalism. Aquarius itself began to ascend around the 1960s, when people became interested in New Age spirituality outside the church ("This is the dawning of the Age of Aquarius" from the musical, Hair), and the Jesus Movement and Charismatic Movement began to spread within the church, as hundreds of thousands of hippies and New Agers found Christ as Savior. They developed a new season of worship music and styles, congregations, and ways of sharing the good news.

As Aquarius continued to ascend (and Pisces to descend), we have had many Spirit-filled revival movements, prophetic movements, and apostolic networks of churches that emphasize the Spirit-filled life. Worship has become more intimate, powerful, and presence-of-God focused, while preaching and teaching has become more real-life and growth-focused, and faith-filled prayer and prophecy have become normal parts of many churches activities.

God is the God of all creation. He is at work in all the world, speaking to people from all backgrounds, beliefs, cultures and understandings, and pushing all things towards the desired goal. There are many people and groups outside of the Christian church who do have some accurate insights into the changing seasons and the coming Aquarian Age, and providing we stay grounded in a proper interpretive framework, we can and should listen to what people are "seeing" and use those insights as bridges to teach or introduce a deeper, more fuller, more Christ-centered understanding of these things. It seems to me that many Biblical prophecies point to what the condition of the world will be (still within time and space, not in some eternal state) as the kingdom of God continues to advance and expand—it indicates a time of universal fullness of the Spirit, peace, health, longevity, harmony, and happiness:

Where no one will say to his neighbor – "know the Lord" – for they shall all know the Lord from the least to the greatest. For I will forgive their iniquity, and their sin I will remember no more..... They will beat their swords into plowshares and their spears into pruning hooks. Nation will not take up sword against nation, nor will they train for war anymore. Everyone will sit under their own vine and under their own fig tree, and no one will make them afraid...The new Jerusalem I make will be full of joy, and her people will be happy. I myself will be filled with joy because of

Jerusalem and her people. There will be no weeping there, no calling for help. Babies will no longer die in infancy, and all people will live out their lifespan. Those who live to be a hundred will be considered young. To die before that would be a sign of punishment. People will build houses and get to live in them—they will not be used by someone else. They will plant vineyards and enjoy the wine—it will not be drunk by others. Like trees, my people will live long lives. They will fully enjoy the things that they have worked for. The work they do will be successful, and their children will not meet with disaster. I will bless them and their descendants for all time to come. Even before they finish praying to me, I will answer their prayers. Wolves and lambs will eat together; lions will eat straw, as cattle do, and snakes will no longer be dangerous, there will be nothing harmful or evil. [Jeremiah 31:31-34; Micah 4:3-4; Isaiah 65:18-24]

All of this is leading up to the "pleroma", the "fullness" at the End of the Ages when God fills all things and when Christ is head over all:

God has now revealed to us his mysterious plan regarding Christ, a plan to fulfill his own good pleasure. And **this is the plan**: *when the times reach their fulfillment, he will bring everything together under the authority of Christ—everything in heaven and on earth.* (Ephesians 1:10-11)

I don't know how you imagine it, but whatever image you hold in your mind, the future is bright, because God is moving in many ways, exposing corruption, inspiring change, increasing our knowledge, working through all people and all creation to lead is onto a brighter, better world—a truly Golden Age. In this current Age we live in, we get the opportunity to *"taste and see that the Lord is good!"* (Psalm 34:8). We get to have a *"foretaste of the powers of the Age to come"* (Hebrews 6:5).

It seems, in the context of the Book of Hebrews (which is all about the very near end of the Old Covenant and its Age, and the full meaning of the Old Covenant symbols and promises as fulfilled spiritually in Christ and in our lives as His followers), the writer is telling his readers that not only should they now totally discard all the trappings of the former Age, and not only should they live in the reality of a new life of faith in Christ in this Age, but he tells them that what they are experiencing in this newly born Age is simply a foretaste of what is to come in the next Age—as the Kingdom is ever-increasing, so their foretaste is destined to increase and enlarge until it blossoms into another, yet future, coming Age where such experiences are normal, commonplace, and part of life.

MISSION ACCOMPLISHED: THE END OF THE AGES

We have looked at the various "Ages" mentioned in scripture, how there are "former Ages" as well as "Ages to come", and how the New Testament deals mainly (though not exclusively) with two Ages (the Old Covenant Age which was passing away and the new Age which was then just beginning) as well as dealing with the "transition period" (also known as the "cusp of the Ages") as the end of one Age and beginning of the next Age overlap for a period of time.

So, what happens when all the Ages come to an end? Do they ever end? Or do they just repeat over and over? The answer is that Ages are part of the cosmic calendar and they are to do with measuring time, and they have both a beginning and an end. Before the creation of our material universe, there was no time—there was eternity—that was "in the beginning" and what the Bible tells us is that "In the beginning, God…" (Genesis 1:1).

Then God went on to "create", and part of that creation was the creation of time (day and night, months and years, seasons and Ages). Only time requires such dualisms as a "beginning" and "ending". So, before time, before the "beginning", there was eternity, and after time has finished, after the "end", there will once again be eternity. I have shown that the word "aionian" is often wrongly translated as "eternal" or "forever", and that the word does not mean eternal at all, but age-enduring. There is an eternal forever, not just for us when we individually die, but for the whole created order. This is a prophecy that awaits future fulfillment—there will come an end of the Ages and thus, an end of time. When that happens, everything in creation will somehow merge—the material dimensions with the spiritual dimensions—all will be one, and God will be **All in All.** (1 Corinthians 15:28).

We will look at some passages from the Bible that speak of this, but just for a bit longer, let's imagine. Imagine that heaven is not up in the sky, but rather in the invisible, spiritual realm which is all around us but beyond our perception. If our eyes were really opened to see the fullness of reality, it would suddenly cause you to see colors, lights, beings, wonder, glory, hear sounds and music, that can only emanate from the presence of God. Not a world a million miles away, but only a thin veil away—a veil that hides this material dimension from that glorious one.

I don't mean to become dualistic myself here by contrasting the material and the spiritual dimensions. On the contrary, I want to show unity and harmony and oneness—that heaven and earth, the material and the spiritual dimensions, are not two separate and isolated realities, in juxtaposition with each other in some way. Not at all. They are one – "Behold, the dwelling of God is with men, and he shall dwell with them and be their God and they shall be his people" (Rev. 21:3). Heaven is all around us, a "great cloud of witnesses" (Heb. 12:1) are all around us; heavenly beings are all around us, lights, colors, and glory that radiates from God's unconditionally loving, joyfully peaceful presence. We just don't see it. We are not yet ready to see it. Our eyes are not fully open.

Some discoveries are being made—about the connections between all living things, the way plants, when wired up to the right equipment, can "sing" and can even respond to humans singing to them and echo their music back to them, or the shared consciousness that schools of fish or flocks of birds can demonstrate as they turn at once and create amazing displays. Our universe is alive and impregnated with the presence of the life of God. Sometimes, some people get glimpses of it. I have had some moments of revelation as a glimpse of that other world which is all around us suddenly breaks in, and God touches my heart and mind in a transformative way.

If our eyes were opened, to quote Elizabeth Barrat Browing – *"Earth's crammed with heaven, And every common bush afire with God; But only he who sees, takes off his shoes – The rest sit round it and pluck blackberries"*—we would see that "every bush is ablaze". Moses' eyes were opened. He saw the blazing glory of that other world shining and burning in a non-destructive way through the bush.

But one day, it will be as if heaven and earth merged into one—our eyes will be opened to see all creation aflame with the glory of God—the whole of creation is divinized, no longer subject to decay, because that is only a phenomenon of time. And what about us? We will be fully God-realized, for want of a better term. I suppose there is a better term in theology; it is called Theosis—the experience of being so fully in union with God, that the two are one—not just in principle, but in experience. That is when "the end shall come".

Remember, "In the beginning, God"? Well, that was the start of time and the Ages. Now, we are at "the end" and what will happen is that "God shall be All in All". I just think that is absolutely mind-boggling and fantastic. It's like the ultimate happy ending to a story. **All is well that ends well—and all shall be well because it will end well.** All creation will be alive and fully animated with the very presence of an unconditionally loving, joyfully peaceful, blissful Father God. For "then comes the End, when God shall be All in All".

REVELATION 21:1-4

I saw "a new heaven and a new earth," for the first heaven and the first earth had passed away, and there was no longer any sea. I saw the Holy City, the new

Jerusalem, coming down out of heaven from God, prepared as a bride beautifully dressed for her husband. And I heard a loud voice from the throne saying, "Look! God's dwelling place is now among the people, and he will dwell with them. They will be his people, and God himself will be with them and be their God. 'He will wipe every tear from their eyes. There will be no more death' or mourning or crying or pain, for the old order of things has passed away."

I CORINTHIANS 15:24-28

Then comes the End, when Jesus delivers the kingdom to God the Father, when He puts an end to all rule and all authority and power. For He must reign till He has put all enemies under His feet. The last enemy that will be destroyed is death… Now when all things are made subject to Him, then the Son Himself will also be subject to God who put all things under Him, so then, God will be All in All.

And so, in the Bible, we see a plan—that all things originate in the One Eternal Original Source—God Himself. And all things shall return to that Source when God shall be all in all. And in-between "Eternity Past" and "Eternity to Come", we see the creation of matter (and the Ages), God gradually and progressively working out His "Plan of the Ages", God's ever-advancing Kingdom growing and spreading until it culminates in the return of Jesus and the final judgment (final, because there is no more judgment, thereafter), or for those of us who die before that "End", we immediately face our final judgment (Hebrews 9:27), bringing "Age-enduring life or Age-enduring punishment". However, that final "End" ushers in the Conclusion of the Ages, when time is no more, when the "eternal now" infuses and is experienced by all creation, and "then God shall be All in All".

Origen of Alexandria (182-254AD)—*When death shall no longer exist, or the sting of death, nor any evil at all, then truly God will be all in all.*

ROMANS 11:36

All things came from Him, and exist through Him, and are returning to Him; to Him is the glory through all the Ages

When we read the scriptures through THEIR eyes, through the eyes of the people who wrote and heard it, when we understand their **culture, customs, and calendar,** we see that a huge change took place 2,000 years ago. It's more than Jesus dying for our sins (which, if that was all it was, would be wonderful in itself). It's about a cosmic change from one Age to another, an upgrade that takes us to a new place in God's plan, and we can never go back to Old Covenant, Old Age thinking that includes legalism, dualism, futurism, and literalism, or else, we may as well build a golden calf.

Part 3:

"If your eyes are focused on the light, your whole being will be flooded with light"

—Jesus, *Luke 11:34*

CHAPTER 14:
FROM UNDER ARREST, TO UNDER A REST

The Old Covenant was established for one "Age" and then it was to pass away and be replaced by "a New and Better Covenant" (Hebrews 8:13). We do not live at the time of the Old Covenant. We don't follow the Old Covenant Laws regarding food, festivals, ceremonies, special holy days, etc. The New Testament is clear on that matter:

MARK 7:19

"Can't you see that the food you put into your body cannot defile you? Food doesn't go into your heart, but only passes through the stomach and then goes into the sewer." (By saying this, Jesus declared that every kind of food is acceptable in God's eyes).

COLOSSIANS 1:16-23

Don't let anyone condemn you for what you eat or drink, or for not celebrating certain holy days or new moon ceremonies or Sabbaths. For these rules are only shadows of the reality yet to come. And Christ himself is that reality...You have died with Christ, and he has set you free from the spiritual powers of this world. So why do you keep on following the rules of the world, such as, "Don't handle! Don't taste! Don't touch!"? Such rules are mere human teachings about things that deteriorate as we use them. These rules may seem wise because they require strong devotion, pious self-denial, and severe bodily discipline. But they provide no help in conquering a person's evil desires.

There is no mixed covenant. We don't live in a mixture of the Old Covenant and the New Covenant. The Old Covenant fully passed away. It's gone, and so are its Laws and rituals. In fact, the truth is that God never wanted an Old Covenant anyway. His aim was always a relationship with humanity. But humanity wasn't ready yet and needed to be educated and prepared.

All around Israel were nations that offered their children in sacrifice to demonic-like gods and goddesses, who kept and mistreated slaves, whose cultures were cruel and brutal. To people who lived in that kind of society, God gave Laws on how to improve society, treat slaves kindly, replace human sacrifice with animal sacrifice, and even treat domestic animals with care and respect. It was the first step-up for humanity. Eventually, both slavery and animal sacrifices would be eradicated, and so would all the Laws.

ROMANS 7:6

But now we have been released from the law, for we died to it and are no longer captive to its power. Now we can serve God, not in the old way of obeying the letter of the law, but in the new way of living in the Spirit.

GOD ORIGINALLY WANTED TO HAVE A RELATIONSHIP WITH THE PEOPLE OF ISRAEL, (AND INVITED THEM UP THE MOUNTAIN TO MEET WITH HIM) BUT THEY ASKED FOR A LAW CODE INSTEAD:

- *And they said to Moses, "You speak to us, and we will listen. But don't let God speak directly to us, or we will die!"* (Exodus 20:19).

GOD ORIGINALLY WANTED TO BE ISRAEL'S KING, BUT THEY ASKED FOR A HUMAN ONE INSTEAD:

- *So all the elders of Israel gathered together and came to Samuel at Ramah. They said to him, "You are old, and your sons do not follow your ways; now appoint a king to lead us, such as all the other nations have." But when they said, "Give us a king to lead us," this displeased Samuel; so he prayed to the Lord. And the Lord told him: "Listen to all that the people are saying to you; it is not you they have rejected, but they have rejected me as their king.* (1 Samuel 8:4-7).

GOD NEVER WANTED ANIMAL SACRIFICES IN THE FIRST PLACE, AS THEY CAN NEVER ATONE FOR SIN, BUT HUMANITY NEEDED A TIME-PERIOD TO GRADUALLY AND PROGRESSIVELY UNDERSTAND THE TRULY LOVING, FATHERLY NATURE OF GOD:

- *"What makes you think I want all your sacrifices?" says the Lord. "I am sick of your burnt offerings of rams and the fat of fattened cattle. I get no pleasure from the blood of bulls and lambs and goats. When you come to worship me, who asked you to parade through my courts with all your ceremony?"* (Isaiah 1:11-13).

- *"It is impossible for the blood of bulls and goats to take away sins."* (Hebrews 10:4).

THE NEW COVENANT THAT JESUS BROUGHT IS NOT ABOUT OBEYING LAWS, OR BEING HARSH WITH YOURSELF, OR MORAL OUTRAGE, OR JUDGING AND CONDEMNING OTHER PEOPLE—IT'S ABOUT GRACE: GOD'S FREE GIFT OFFERED TO ALL, AND THEN DISCOVERING YOUR TRUE PURPOSE WHICH GOD PREPARED FOR YOU, AND PURSUING THAT:

- *"And God raised us up with Christ and seated us with him in the heavenly realms in Christ Jesus, in order that in the COMING AGES he might show the incomparable riches of his grace, expressed in his kindness to us in Christ Jesus. For it is by GRACE you have been saved, through faith— and this is not from yourselves, it is the gift of God—not by works, so that no one can boast. For we are God's handiwork, created in Christ Jesus to do good works, which God PREPARED IN ADVANCE for us to do."* (Ephesians 2:6-10)

Once you discover just how huge the transition was from Old to New Covenants, and that it was predicted in prophetic scripture and even written in the heavenly constellations that the old order would fully and finally pass away (and with it, its Laws, priesthood, ceremonies, and festivals) and a brand new order would be ushered in (based on the offer of a free gift of forgiveness of sins, eternal life, relationship with God as Father, and ongoing and growing spiritual experience of the Holy Spirit), you can never go back; you can never be duped again by people saying that you need to literally observe and obey passages in the Old Testament—you don't.

You shouldn't. You would be simply doing what the Israelites did when they made a golden calf; you would be attempting to live under an Age which has fully and finally passed away. You are not supposed to live in guilt and condemnation as if you are constantly "under arrest" for breaking one of Gods' Laws. You should be living "under a rest", resting in the Finished Work of Christ. He did it all, and He said, "It is finished!".

HEBREWS 4:9-10

There remains, then, a Sabbath-rest for the people of God. For anyone who enters God's rest also rests from their works, just as God did from his.

The relevance that the Old Testament has for us now is that it contains types and shadows of the full revelation of the New Covenant. We now read and meditate upon the Old Testament, not so we can follow its Laws and rituals, but as an "allegory" that serves as an "example" to us:

GALATIANS 4:22-24

*It is written that Abraham had two sons: the one by a bondwoman, the other by a freewoman. But he who was of the bondwoman was born according to the flesh, and he of the freewoman through promise, and these things are an **ALLEGORY**. For these are the two covenants.*

I CORINTHIANS 10:2-11

They (the Israelites) *were all baptized into Moses…Now, these things occurred as **EXAMPLES to US**…These things happened to them as **EXAMPLES** and were written down as warnings for US…*

CHAPTER 15:
ONCE YOU SEE IT!

If I said to you, "I will meet you again in two weeks", you would rightly take my statement to be a comment about a FUTURE plan, something that is yet to happen. However, if you were reading an account of me talking to someone 15 years ago, and I then said to them "I will meet you again in two weeks", you would presume that the meeting had already taken place, 15 years ago. The fact that I am speaking in the future tense ("I will meet you…") doesn't change a thing—you understand that it was future-tense when I said it because the meeting had not yet taken place, but that it is now past tense.

Jesus spoke of a time of "great tribulation" that would happen in Judea and especially the city of Jerusalem. He said that armies would surround the city, and it would be destroyed, and not a single stone of the Temple would be left standing. Not that Jesus wanted this to happen, He clearly didn't (see Matthew 23:37), but they would not listen. Then He told us when that would happen—"this generation will not pass away until all these things have taken place".

I just can't understand how people can pick up a Bible and read that and then claim that THIS generation, the one we are currently living in, won't pass away until these things take place. I understand Jesus is speaking of a future event, but like my "two weeks from now" example, that future event (future to Him and His hearers) is now a past event (to us). It has been fulfilled—it was HIS generation He was speaking about, not ours. It really doesn't take an expert in reading comprehension to understand that—it does take a lot of help to misunderstand it, and unfortunately, many people have "helped" us in that way.

I understand the appeal of **Futurism.** It's exciting and a bit scary and like being in a movie to believe that any minute now, great and amazing events will unfold on this planet—an antichrist, a tribulation, signs in the sky, earth-changing events in nature, high-tech wars, millions of people vanishing without an explanation, etc. Yes, it sounds exciting and dramatic and urgent, but none of it is what the Bible actually teaches.

Do you want to truly UNDERSTAND the Bible? Or do you want to deliberately MISUNDERSTAND the Bible because that makes it sound more exciting? If your goal is to genuinely understand scripture, then read it in **context!** If it says that a prophecy is "about to be fulfilled" or "will happen soon" or "will come to past shortly" or that "the time has come" or that "this generation"—the ones being spoken to would actually see the fulfillment, then that's what it means! No need to do interpretative gymnastics to try and explain the context away—accept the context. It's the TRUTH that sets you free, not a comic-book version of reality.

It is actually much more exciting to discover that most prophecy is already fulfilled. It strengthens your faith when you read a prophecy delivered by Jesus, which He says will be fulfilled within a generation, and then to read history, like *The War of the Jews* by Flavius Josephus, (who was an eye-witness to the events of 70 AD) and read the two descriptions side by side and be amazed at how accurate and specific Jesus' prophecy was.

The antidote to **Futurism** (to reading all Biblical prophecy as if you are still waiting for them to happen) is to read Biblical prophecies in their original context, (so you know what it actually predicts), and read history (so you know when it was fulfilled). When you have "seen" that the tribulation, Beast, anti-christs, and destruction of the Temple are now fulfilled and past, you can never "un-see" it again.

CHAPTER 16:
IT AIN'T NECESSARILY SO

I have heard all sorts of ridiculous statements made by good people who think they are defending the integrity of scripture, but who are actually making it even harder to believe the fairy-tale-like versions of Biblical stories that evolve from overly literalistic interpretations. I have heard people say, "Some people find it hard to believe that Jonah was swallowed by a whale, but I would believe that the whale was swallowed by Jonah if the Bible said it, because the Bible is true and every man is a liar!" That statement (and the numerous statements that are like that, claiming that people should "just believe" the Bible without even engaging their brains, or trying to actually understand the Bible) does more to put people off the Bible, drive them away from what they see as blind, cult-like naivety, than it ever will to encourage people to actually engage with scripture.

It seems that the more outlandish or extreme or contrary to the normal laws of nature a claim is, the more important it is for people to accept it as "literal". I have noticed that atheists tend to quote the Bible "literally" in the same way that Fundamentalists do because that's the easiest way for them to criticize it. I also notice that they don't treat other ancient documents like that, but seek to understand what the ancient writers were trying to communicate.

The problem is, no one reads other literature in that manner. If you are reading a dictionary or encyclopedia, you won't read it like a novel, (from cover to cover, expecting some kind of storyline). No, you would read it as a reference book—one that you look to for a definition or explanation of something, not as a storybook. You would read a cookery book, a book of poetry, a history book, a novel, and a science book all in different ways.

If you read a love-poem which said "when my eyes saw you, Cupids arrows struck my heart, and it exploded", you would never conclude that there is a literal Cupid that caused the author of the poem to have a heart attack! You would never try to prove something scientific from that statement. You KNOW it's using symbolic language—it's poetry, after all. Well, the Bible contains lots of poetry, parables, stories, narratives, history, allegory, apocalypses, dreams, and visions. It contains lots of different kinds of literature, and you don't read it all the same.

Here is an example: many Christians argue that the world was created around 6,000 years ago in 6 consecutive 24 hour days. How do they arrive at that conclusion? By treating family trees and a common piece of Ancient Near-Eastern poetry as if they are teaching modern-day science. By ripping what they are reading out of its original context and genre of literature and making it into a completely different genre of literature. By doing exactly the thing I gave an example of regarding Cupid.

They will get out a calculator and add up all the ages of people in Biblical genealogies to work out how many years ago Adam lived. The problem with that method is that ancient people were not writing scientifically valid genealogies so that people who are obsessed by dates—thousands of years later—would be able to calculate a date. No, they were recording family lines and emphasizing important figures. They didn't even record all of their ancestors—for example, by comparing the genealogy in Matthew chapter 1 with the genealogies in the Old Testament, we discover that Matthew omitted Ahaziah, Joash, and Amaziah. These passages show that the word "begat" skips generations, so how do we know that other genealogies in the Bible haven't likewise done so? We have no idea how many people were dropped out of genealogies and how far back they really go.

The second issue with this idea is that the Bible doesn't say the "six days of creation" (or "seven days" if you include the day of rest) was when the earth came into existence. If you read the account carefully, the earth already existed at the start of these six days—we only see God "separating" things in creation (light from dark, water from land, plants from animals, male from female, etc.).

The creation happened in the dateless past; we were told not when or how, but simply, *"In the beginning God created the heavens and the earth"*. (Genesis 1:1). Then, we were given a poem where all of God's creative acts are put in the template of a regular week—that's what the 7 days account is—a Hebrew poem! Not a scientific account. I am not down-grading it in any way; I am rescuing a piece of inspired poetry from interpreters who want to rip it out of context and genre and read it as if it's a secular science book. I don't "take the Bible literally", I "take it seriously", too seriously to ignore genre and context.

It was actually a practice in the Ancient Near-East to write a poem or song that depicted all the heroic acts of a king as having happened in a one-week period. "On the first day, he conquered the Ethiopians; on the second day, he subdued Egypt; on the third…and on the seventh day, he reclined on his throne and received tribute from all his con-quered territories". That kind of thing. Genesis is saying "God created everything, He created in successive stages, and He created it for man to inhabit" and that truth was depicted in a common way—as a seven-day poem of the greatness of the king.

One of the huge things we misunderstand is the idioms that the Bible employs, which were common to their day but are mysteries to us. We use idioms today. As I mentioned earlier, we may say *"it's raining cats and dogs"* or *"my feet are killing me"* but no one thinks we mean that literally; we know these are idioms and figures of speech. The Bible contains lots of Aramaic idioms—figures of speech that were common amongst the various Aramaic cultures.

But I suppose that it doesn't really matter which of these events were literal or not; their true purpose is to remain as a lasting allegorical story containing deep spiritual truth. Take the story of Abraham and Sarah and Hagar found in Genesis from chapters 12-24, regardless of its historicity (which I fully accept); its lasting purpose is as an allegory for us:

GALATIANS 4:22-26

It is written that Abraham had two sons: the one by a bondwoman, the other by a freewoman. But he who was of the bondwoman was born according to the flesh, and he of the freewoman through promise, and these things are an **ALLEGORY**. *For these are the two covenants: the one from Mount Sinai which gives birth to bondage, which is Hagar—for this Hagar is Mount Sinai in Arabia, and corresponds to Jerusalem which now is, and is in bondage with her children—but the Jerusalem above is free, which is the mother of us all.*

Or what about that great historic event (and I certainly do believe it actually happened in time and in history) that we call the Exodus? What is the purpose of that story? So we can argue about whether or not it is historical? No, its lasting value to Christians is as an allegory for us; it's a story with a lesson for us today—that's its lasting importance:

I CORINTHIANS 10:1-11

I do not want you to be ignorant of the fact, brothers and sisters, that our ancestors were all under the cloud and that they all passed through the sea. They were all baptized into Moses in the cloud and in the sea. They all ate the same spiritual food and drank the same spiritual drink; for they drank from the spiritual rock that accompanied them, and that rock was Christ…Now these things occurred as **EXAMPLES** *to keep US from setting our hearts on evil things as they* *did…These things happened to them as* **EXAMPLES** *and were written down as warnings for US, on whom the overlap of the Ages has come.*

Or what about those who take the Book of Revelation to be a literal account of the future, written in advance? Will there really be a giant Godzilla emerge from the Mediterranean Sea? (Rev. 13) Is there really a pregnant woman flying around in outer space being chased by a hungry dragon? (Rev 12). No, Revelation is an apocalypse, which was a particular genre of writing, where prophecies regarding the flow of history are depicted in symbolic language (dragons and beasts being empires and rulers etc.). The Book of Revelation talks about the fall of Babylon, the Great City—should we take that literally? Is it a rebuilt Babylon in the modern country of Iraq? It tells us exactly what it is, Babylon is used as—you've guessed it—an ALLEGORY. An allegory of the corrupt city of Jerusalem in the first century AD, which would be destroyed by the Romans (the Beast) in AD 70, and they would burn the city with fire:

REVELATION 11:8 & 17:3-6

The great city which is ALLEGORICALLY called Sodom and Egypt, where their Lord was crucified…… Then the angel carried me away in the Spirit into a wilderness. There I saw a woman (*natural, physical Jerusalem) *sitting on a scarlet beast* (*Rome and its emperor) *that was covered with blasphemous names and had seven heads and ten horns* (*Roman governmental districts and Caesars). *The woman was dressed in purple and scarlet, and was glittering with gold, precious stones and pearls. She held a golden cup in her hand, filled with abominable things and the filth of her adulteries. The name written on her forehead was a mystery: BABYLON the GREAT, the mother of harlots and of the abominations of the earth. I saw that the woman was drun*k with the blood of God's holy people, the blood of those who bore testimony to Jesus.

You see, it's too important to "take it literally", it's not enough to "believe" the Bible, it's important to actually "understand" it. And much of it is written in parables, allegories, and symbolic language.

CHAPTER 17:
SPIRITUAL, BUT NOT RELIGIOUS

"Theologians and physicians have never quite gotten down to the fact that this is a singular Universe. It will be a great day for the world when they do. Preachers still insist that it is a duo-verse; that there is a devil who is nearly or quite as strong as God; and doctors believe in disease as an entity; a real evil which has power in itself. But Jesus pointed out that there is no devil who is apparent in nature. It is your Father, said he, who makes the sun shine and sends the rain; who clothes the grass of the field and feeds the birds. This is God's world. The devil cannot make the sun rise or set. He cannot stop the grass from growing or starve the birds; he has not as much power as a scarecrow; he cannot keep the crows out of the corn" **Wallace Wattles. (Author: 1860-1911)**

It's becoming more and more common to hear people say they are "spiritual but not religious". I understand why. I have said it myself. Sometimes, we get so jaded by the negative, critical, judgmental attitudes of religious people that we want to draw as far away as possible. The problem is, we are still left with an unfulfilled spiritual dimension to our lives. We still crave God, and life, and love, and guidance, and fulfillment—spiritual things.

In many ways, Jesus never intended to found a religion, but to bring a new way of spiritual connection with God for all people in all places. In Jesus day, there was a religious dispute between two different "denominations"—the Jews had their Temple in Jerusalem, and the Samaritans had a rival Temple at Mount Gerizim. Jesus once met with a woman at Samaria and revealed that the new Age that He was ushering in would be a "spiritual but not religious" Age—one concerned with a living experience of God, not rituals and duties:

JOHN 4:4-25

"Jesus had to go through Samaria on the way. Eventually he came to the Samaritan village of Sychar, near the field that Jacob gave to his son Joseph. Jacob's well was there; and Jesus, tired from the long walk, sat wearily beside the well about noontime. Soon, a Samaritan woman came to draw water, and Jesus said to her, "Please give me a drink." He was alone at the time because his disciples had gone into the village to buy some food.

The woman was surprised, for Jews refuse to have anything to do with Samaritans. She said to Jesus, "You are a Jew, and I am a Samaritan woman. Why are you asking me for a drink?" Jesus replied, "If you only knew the gift God has for you and who you are speaking to, you would ask me, and I would give you living water." "But sir, you don't have a rope or a bucket," she said, "and this well is very deep. Where would you get this living water? And besides, do you think you're greater than our ancestor Jacob, who gave us this well? How can you offer better water than he and his sons and his animals enjoyed?"

Jesus replied, "Anyone who drinks this water will soon become thirsty again. But those who drink the water I give will never be thirsty again. It becomes a fresh, bubbling spring within them, giving them eternal life." "Please, sir," the woman said, "give me this water! Then I'll never be thirsty again, and I won't have to come here to get water." "Go and get your husband," Jesus told her. "I don't have a husband," the woman replied. Jesus said, "You're right! You don't have a husband—for you have had five husbands, and you aren't even married to the man you're living with now. You certainly spoke the truth!" "Sir," the woman said, "you must be a prophet. So tell me, why is it that you Jews insist that Jerusalem is the only place of worship, while we Samaritans claim it is here at Mount Gerizim, where our ancestors worshiped?"

Jesus replied, "Believe me, dear woman, the time is coming when it will no longer matter whether you worship the Father on this mountain or in Jerusalem. You Samaritans know very little about the one you worship, while we Jews know all about him, for salvation comes through the Jews. But the time is coming—indeed it's here now—when true worshipers will worship the Father in spirit and in truth. The Father is looking for those who will worship him that way. For God is Spirit, so those who worship him must worship in spirit and in truth." The woman said, "I know the Messiah is coming—the one who is called Christ. When he comes, he will explain everything to us." Then Jesus told her, "I am the Messiah!"

- **God is Spirit!** He is not an old man in the sky or a judge on a throne far away. He is here, with us, amongst us, invisibly present everywhere. He is the life-force that animates all things. *"For in him we live and move and have our being".* (Acts 17:28)

- **God doesn't live in a Temple—He lives in YOU!** *"Don't you realize that you yourselves are the temple of God and that the Spirit of God lives in you?"* (1 Corinthians 3:16)

- **So, God dwells everywhere, including within us, and He is a good God**—full of love and light and life, with no dark aspect to His nature: *"This is the message we have heard from him and declare to you: God is light; in him there is no darkness at all...we know and rely on the love God has for us. God is love. Whoever lives in love lives in God, and God in them."* (1 John 1:5 & 4:16)

- **God never changes—He is always the same,** (not in the sense of being boring or uneventful, but in the sense of being consistent and trustworthy). *"I am the LORD, and I do not change...Jesus Christ is the same yesterday and today and forever...Every good and perfect gift is from above, coming down from the Father of the heavenly lights, who does not change like shifting shadows."* (Malachi 3:6; Hebrews 13:8; James 1:17).

Although He never changes, He relates to us in different ways at different times. God often likens Himself to a parent (usually, a Father but on some occasions, as a Mother. See Hosea 11:3-4; 13:8; Isaiah 66:13; 49:15; 42:14; Psalm 131:2, etc.). If you are a parent, imagine the different ways you relate to your child at various stages of their growth.

First, you have to do everything for them, then you gradually and progressively teach them to do things for themselves while you supervise and protect, but your eventual goal is for them to become mature and able to navigate the world because their understanding has grown. They are still, and always will be, your child, but they have grown, and the manner in which you relate to them has matured.

It's the same with God and humanity. He began by treating us like little children who knew nothing and needed to be told everything. Then He sent prophets and teachers and sages to help mature our understanding of God and His plan. He gradually and progressively removed wrong beliefs and added correct new beliefs, (this is called Progressive Revelation by Biblical scholars—God didn't tell us everything at once but gradually and progressively educated us), until the time of Jesus—the FULL revelation of God. Jesus is "the Word of God made flesh" (John 1:14).

Jesus is "the visible image of the invisible God" (Colossians 1:15); Jesus is the one who said, "if you have seen me, you have seen the Father" (John 14:9). If you want to know what God is like, don't look to Moses, or Elijah, or David—look at Jesus.

If you want to understand God through the stories and writings and journey of faith that Moses or Elijah or David went through, make sure you don't fall into one of the four traps of legalism, literalism, futurism, or dualism. Instead, see their stories as an "allegory" that is written as an "example" for you, and make sure that you at least try to understand their **culture**, their **calendar**, and their **customs**, as that will resolve all four of these problems in one go!

God is Love, Light, Life, Spirit, and He is good. And there is no rival or competing presence anywhere in creation—*"I am the Lord your God and besides me there is no other!"* (Isaiah 45:5). How many "others" are there? None.

Christianity is going through a significant shift, from simply "believing" a set of doctrines, to actually "experiencing" the God we claim to believe in. We are finally getting around to emphasizing the relational aspect of faith, the experiential aspect of God. In the Bible, the word "know" means "experiential knowledge". For example, Adam "knew" his wife Eve and she conceived. He didn't just know about her, he "knew" her intimately. When the Bible says that we can know God and know the truth and know Christ, it is saying that we can genuinely, truly, experience the ever-present Spirit of God at work in and through us. We are going from simply being "Bible-believing Christians" to being "Spirit-filled Christians"—people who don't simply read about others experiences of God and believe them, but people who hunger and thirst to experience the things we are reading about.

When I discovered the ancient **calendar** that the Hebrews used, and how it made the things being discussed in the Bible much clearer, it caused me to look deeper into their **culture** and **customs** to see what else I was misunderstanding. It became clear that some passages that I had been taking literally were actually filled with metaphors and imagery that was common at the time and meant something very different to how I was reading it. I saw how **Literalism** was causing me to actually misunderstand the Bible, and how such Literalism led to a **Legalistic** approach to scripture, which pushed God's Kingdom off into the **Future** sometime and caused us to believe that we are living in a **Dualistic** nightmare of a world, controlled by the devil.

How freeing it was to discover that God knows what He is doing, has a "plan of the Ages", and is gradually and progressively advancing His Kingdom everywhere—His new world which is emerging amongst us more and more as we adopt His new way of living. The truth shall set you free.

If only we could get away from overly **Literal** interpretations of scripture and actually discover what the Bible meant to the original audience—in their culture, customs, and calendar—then our minds would expand, our vision would increase, and our faith would become richer, fuller, and deeper. **And we can**—if we read scripture in its original context.

If only we could get away from **Legalistic** rules and judgments, guilt and shame, and focus instead on growing, maturing, and changing on the inside as we open up more to a genuine relationship with God. **And we can**—because the Law code fully passed away at the End of the Age.

If only we could get away from the black-and-white **Dualistic** thinking that legalism produces, and see ALL of life as a gift from God and ALL of creation as under the direction of the one true, loving God. **And we can**—because God came "in the flesh" to show that He isn't far away from His creation, and through His Finished Work, Jesus completely defeated all evil, and now, there is only one King and one Kingdom.

If only we could get away from fearing the **Future** and expecting persecution, hostility and disaster, and instead, saw a bright future promised by God. **And we can**—because once we see that the tribulation, Beasts, and End of the Age happened 2,000 years ago, we can focus on the advancing Kingdom of God.

How should all of this affect our lives and our Christian faith? When these ideas truly begin to integrate within you, it's the start of living free and fulfilled, enjoying life to the full, like Jesus promised (John 10:0). It is also the start of being able to clear up the confusion that so many Christians live under. They have lots of pieces of Biblical knowledge, but don't see how they fit together. They have all the pieces of the jigsaw puzzle but don't have the picture on the front of the box, and so have to guess what the picture should be. It's actually worse than that, many have been shown a wrong picture, and struggle as they may, they cannot get the pieces they have (their knowledge of scripture, their experiences of the Holy Spirit) to fit the faulty picture of a legalistic, dualistic mixed-covenant Christianity that they have been shown—and they think there is something wrong with them, and they have to try harder.

Now you can lay aside any anxiety or confusion you had about "the end times" and the antichrist and the number of the Beast. You know what that was about, you can marvel at the accurate fulfilment of Jesus prophecy and the veracity of the Word of God, and let those passages strengthen your faith in the God who keeps His Word, rather than cause anxiety and confusion over an uncertain future, because you know that God has a plan, He knows what He is doing, and Age to Age His plan is progressing and His Kingdom increasing, and all will end well when God shall be All, and in All.

You live in the time in-between the End of the Age at Jesus time and the return of Christ in our future. That long period of time when we are to keep filled up with the oil of the Spirit, discover, use, and not neglect our God-given gifts and talents, reign in life as seated in heavenly places with Christ, far above being bothered by some defeated devil, principalities or powers. So enjoy your life! Enjoy your faith. Enjoy prayer, and God's free gift of grace which is yours, regardless of your performance. Discover your gifts and unique identity, and put them to fruitful use. You will find personal fulfillment as you fulfill your true life purpose.

Walk in nature and enjoy God's creation, not only in the day but at night. Look up at the stars, let their light bathe your soul, and know that the God who created such a precise time clock has everything going according to plan—you just need to come into alignment with his plan for you. And when you read the Bible, don't leap to fantastical conclusions if something is obscure. Think about the **context** and who was speaking to whom. Think about the **calendar,** and when in God's plan of the Ages it took place. Think about their **customs** and **culture,** and put yourself in their mindset.

So how are we to live our lives? Not worrying about or preparing for the End of Days, nor judging others (or ourselves) for how far along they (or we) are on the journey of growth. Nor neglecting to enjoy the gift of life that God has given us by becoming spiritually intense. We are to live in a growing relationship with God, one in which He works in us developing growth, character, maturity and anointing (keeping our oil lamps full and burning—Matthew 25:1-13) and discovering and using our God given gifts and talents and putting them to good use in our unique life purpose (multiplying our talents—Matthew 25:14-29).

That's how the Kingdom advances—the Kingdom expands within us as our relationship with God deepens and it advances through us as we do the things God has created us to do with the gifts and talents he has given us. The Kingdom will advance throughout all succeeding Ages, until the End comes when Jesus hands the Kingdom back to the Farther, and God is All in All. In this Age, in our own lives, let's live lives that are full of Gods' Spirit, and let's also live lives that are full and abundant. Let's expect miracles through faith and reach for a greater manifestation of the powers of the Age to come, but let's not become superficial and gullible. Let's love people, and eating and drinking, and walking and sleeping and living; let's live fully and freely, under-guarded by a deep and growing relationship with Christ. Let's see God at work in everything and everyone, working out his long term plan of the Ages.

Let's live with our eyes wide open

For Further Study

Astrological Imagery and the Ages in the Bible

JOB 38:31-33 – GOD SPEAKS TO JOB

"Can you direct the movement of the stars—binding the cluster of the Pleiades or loosening the cords of Orion? Can you direct the constellations through the seasons or guide the Bear with her cubs across the heavens? Do you know the laws of the universe? Can you use them to regulate the earth?"

The word for "constellations" used here is "Mazzaroth" – It is the Hebrew term for the twelve constellations of the zodiac. Notice that the other constellations (not just the 12) are mentioned – Pleiades, Orion, (who is the 'messianic figure' in ancient Egyptian mythology), the Great Bear and its cubs – and notice that their influence "regulates the earth". For example, the moon "regulates" the sea tides; so, it's not a stretch to see how the heavenly bodies do some influence on the earth.

In Ezekiel, we see an apocalyptic vision of the "likeness of the glory of God" (chapter 1), and it is shown as Four Living Beings, with four faces – that of a man (Aquarius), a bull (Taurus), a lion (Leo), and an eagle (Scorpio – of rather, Ophiuchus the serpent holding eagle, the major star above Scorpio that is swooping down to destroy it's "sting"). These are the four fixed points of the zodiac, as well as the four elements of the ancient world (Air, Water, Fire, and Earth). As well as these constellations being represented in apocalyptic visions/writings (like Ezekiel's four living creatures, Revelations symbol-pictures, and Job's dialogue with God), once our eyes are open to them, we start to see how "Ages-thinking" saturated everything in that ancient culture, and influences many of the (to us) more obscure passages in scripture in a more allegorical way. For example:

In Numbers, we see that the "twelve tribes of Israel" are encamped around the tabernacle in the form that the 12 "houses" of the zodiac were envisioned to be camped around the sun. The sun would symbolically "pass through" each of the "twelve houses" of the constellations, and "the Angel of the Lord" was said to pass through the camp where the twelve houses or tribes of Israel were placed. Each tribe had a banner with a heraldic symbol on it, and those symbols correspond with the twelve constellations. Some of the pictures are similar, and some are different to the pictures that we use today in our constellations, but those where the picture-symbols which THEY used at that time. (See Numbers 2).

In Exodus 28, we see that the High Priest's garments included a breastplate which contained twelve different gemstones, one to represent each of the tribes of Israel. Interestingly, those twelve stones are the twelve "birthstones" which each correspond to the twelve constellations of the zodiac.

In Revelation, as well as the constellations previously mentioned, we see this picture of the "heavenly Jerusalem" and it has "twelve gates" (the twelve gates or houses of the zodiac) and each gate is a pearl (symbolizing the moon, which passes through each gate), there is a river of life (Aquarius), and there are twelve foundation stones—the same twelve stones that were in the High Priest's breastplate. These are 12 birthstones of the zodiac, and they are listed in reverse order from the usual order—that's because they are symbolizing the Ages, which happen in reverse order to the monthly/annual order of the zodiac (that's why it's called the "PREcession of the Equinoxes and not the PROcession, because the zodiac go in a cycle one way each year, with each constellation providing one month, but they go through the Ages of the Great Year in exactly the opposite order)—that's why we know for sure it is speaking of the Ages. In Rev. 6:2, we see Sagittarius; in 6:5, we see Libra; in 14:14, we see the Decan Bootes who is a crowned man harvesting with a sickle. Also in chapter 12, we see Virgo and Draco…and we could go on through the book.

In Genesis 28, we see Jacod having a dream of a ladder to heaven in which "the angels were ascending and descending". To the ancients, each of the stars was represented by an angel (or vice versa). In one of CS Lewis's Narnia books, *The Voyage of the Dawn Treader*, Eustice meets an angelic-like being who is a "star". "In our world," says Eustace, "a star is a huge ball of flaming gas." "Even in your world, my son," (says the Star), "that is not what a star is, but only what it is made of"—that is an idea from the ancient world. Stars are personified. The angels ascending and descending symbolize (at least in part) the constellations of the Ages ascending and descending. That sheds a bit more light on what Jesus meant when He said: "You will see heaven opened, and the angels of God ascending and descending on the Son of Man" (John 1:51). Meaning, "it is with me—in my ministry, life, death, and resurrection—that one Age will descend, and a new Age will ascend—this is the cusp of the Ages, and a new Age is being born".

Allegories are shown, like Jonah being swallowed by a "great fish" (Pisces) and kept in its belly for three days and nights, before being spat onto the land to bring God's message to the people of Nineveh (non-Israelites) who then repent and receive his message. This is a foretaste of the Piscean Age, which was birthed in the death and resurrection of Jesus: "No sign will be given to this generation, except the sign of the prophet Jonah. For as Jonah was in the belly of the great fish for three days and three nights, so will the Son of Man be in the heart of the earth for three days and three nights", (Matthew 12:40). And this leads to God's word being preached to all nations (not just Israel), who will gladly accept the message. (Notice that it is the "sign" of Jonah—the story contains a "sign", a "symbol", an "allegory" in picture form).

Another allegory is seen in Jesus telling His disciples, "As you enter the city, a man carrying a jar of water will meet you. Follow him to the house that he enters". (Luke 22:10). It was very unusual to see a man carrying a bucket of water—it was a chore or job that was normally, in that culture, given to women and children. All through the Bible, we see stories of women going to a well to fetch water. But they would see a man carrying water (symbolizing Aquarius) and they were to "follow him", and he would take them to a "house" and when they went, they entered an "upper room" where "everything will be prepared". This allegorically and symbolically speaks of Jesus sending us into the Aquarian Age to be taken to a higher place to enjoy God's feast which is prepared.

Lastly, Paul uses some interesting astronomical terms in Romans 8:38-39, he says "nothing in all creation can separate us from the love of God", and he mentions dualistic opposites (dualism is what makes us feel "separate" from God, so dualistic experiences can create that feeling of separateness, but he says that even these apparent dualisms cannot separate us from God's love—God remains the same). Paul says:

"I am convinced that neither death nor life, neither angels nor demons, neither the present nor the future, neither height nor depth, nor any-thing else in all creation, will be able to separate us from the love of God that is in Christ Jesus our Lord."

Those words "height nor depth" are actually (in the original Greek) astronomical terms which mean "neither what is ascending nor what is descending"—in other words, regardless of which Age we are in, or in Paul's case, even in the transition period between two Ages, when one is ascending, and one is descending, God's constant love remains un-changed.

The Ages may change, but God doesn't. Now, think of that when you sing worship songs which speak of the Ages: "You stay the same through the Ages, your love never changes"; "Age to Age He stands, and time is in His hands, the beginning and the end".

I TIMOTHY 1:17

"All honour and glory to God until the fulness of the Ages! For He is the King of the Ages, invisible, immortal, and who alone is God."

I CORINTHIANS 2:6-8

"We do, however, speak a message of wisdom among the mature, but not the wisdom of this Age or of the rulers of this Age, who are coming to nothing. No, we declare God's wisdom, a mystery that has been hidden and that God destined for our glory before the time of the Ages. None of the rulers of this Age understood it, for if they had, they would not have crucified the Lord of glory". Paul is saying to his readers that there is an Age which is "coming to nothing", its "rulers are coming to nothing" and it was the rulers of this Age who "crucified the Lord of glory"—that is clearly also talking about the passing-away Age, the coming-to-nothing Age, the "obsolete Age"—it was the Old Covenant "rulers" who had Jesus crucified.

MATTHEW 28:19-20

"Go and make disciples of all nations, baptizing them in the name of the Father and of the Son and of the Holy Spirit, and teaching them to obey everything I have commanded you. And surely I am with you always, to the very end of the age.' It seems to me that Jesus is talking about the newly arriving Age here. He is sending His disciples out to preach the gospel, the good news, and teach people about Jesus. It is the commission that lasts for the entirety of the Age, and Jesus promises His continual presence "until the end of the Age"—not the end of the world, nor the end

of the "passing away Age" of the Old Covenant. He isn't talking about the Old Covenant; in context, He is talking about the message of the gospel and how it is to be preached everywhere—that's the world of THIS current Age that we are still in, and Jesus is still with us.

MATTHEW 12:32

"Anyone who speaks against the Holy Spirit will not be forgiven, neither in this age nor in the age to come".

Jesus is saying "neither in this current, dying, Old Covenant Age of Aires, nor in the coming Age of Pisces". (But He never says whether this sin can be forgiven in yet future ages).

HEBREWS 6:4-5

"It is impossible for those who have once been enlightened, who have tasted the heavenly gift, who have shared in the Holy Spirit, who have tasted the goodness of the word of God and the powers of the coming age…"

The New Covenant will continue forever, and the Kingdom of God will never stop increasing, regardless of which Age it is. But each Age takes us one step closer to the fullness on the Kingdom. There is so much more to come—we only have a taste at this time.

It is interesting that the only Jewish sect that Jesus doesn't criticize in the gospels are the Essenes. We know from the Dead Sea Scrolls that the Essenes knew that they were living in the time of the end of the Age and they were expecting the Messiah to arrive any time. They had calculated this using their calendar of the Ages (and so they knew the Age was descending), and also by calculating the prophecy in Daniel where he predicted that the Messiah would arrive in "70 weeks" (weeks of years, not weeks of days—so, 490 years—Daniel 9). Because both their astronomical calendar and Daniel's prophecy collated so well, they knew they were in the time of the "end of the Age", and they had even calculated what some have called "the messiah's horoscope". They calculated the position in the sky of the various constellations which would need to be in place for the end of one Age, the beginning of another, and the coming of the Messiah. They were living in a time when two Ages were "overlapping"—if we can imagine Ages to be like pieces of rope—each one with a starting point and a finishing point, and if we overlap the end of rope, one, and the beginning of rope, two, that piece which is overlapped, where TWO ENDS COME TOGETHER—that is the transition, the cusp, the overlap of the Ages:

I CORINTHIANS 10:11

Now these things were written down for our instruction, on whom the ends of the Ages has come.

So, the New Testament period (the life, teaching, and ministry of Jesus/Apostles/Early Church) happened during the TRANSITION PERIOD as the Old Covenant Age was passing away and the New Covenant Age had just been born or was "dawning". Both Covenants/Ages co-existed side-by-side for one generation, and that is why we still see some Law-Grace mix going on in the New Testament itself. There is all this teaching about how salvation is by grace, not by works, and how the Law and its curse and punishments have passed away—yet, we see a few Old-Testament-like events—Ananias & Sapphira struck dead, Herod smote by an angel, a wizard being struck blind, (see Acts 5:1, 12:23, 13:8). All of those people were still connected to Old Covenant Israel (not a gentile amongst them, and even although Herod was an Edomite, he had aligned himself with the Jews and became king of Judea). After AD 70, however, the final "passing away" of the entire Old Covenant system took place, within "one generation" as Jesus predicted, and now we live ONLY in grace, with no law, and no Old Covenant left:

REVELATION 15:3

Just and true are your ways, King of the AGES.

I TIMOTHY 1:17

Now to the King of the Ages, immortal, invisible, to God who alone is wise, be honor and glory throughout all the Ages. Amen.

Why Legalism is Dangerous to your Spiritual Health

The law is an unbearable yoke. (Acts 15:10)

The law reveals sin but cannot fix it. (Romans 3:20)

If the law worked, then faith would be irrelevant. (Romans 4:14)

The law brings wrath upon those who follow it. (Romans 4:15)

The purpose of the law was to increase sin. (Romans 5:20)

Christians are not under the law. (Romans 6:14)

Christians have been delivered from the law. (Romans 7:1-6)

The law is good, perfect, and holy, but cannot help you be good, perfect or holy. (Rom 7:7-12)

The law which promises life only brings death through sin. (Romans 7:10)

The law makes you sinful beyond measure. (Romans 7:13)

The law is weak. (Romans 8:2-3)

The strength of sin is the law (1 Corinthians 15:56)

The law is a ministry of death. (2 Corinthians 3:7)

The law is a ministry of condemnation. (2 Corinthians 3:9)

The law has faded away. (2 Corinthians 3:11)

Anywhere the law is preached, it produces a heart-hardening veil. (2 Corinthians 3:14-15)

The law justifies nobody. (Galatians 2:16)

Christians are dead to the law. (Galatians 2:19)

The law frustrates grace. (Galatians 2:21)

To go back to the law after embracing faith is "stupid". (Galatians 3:1)

The law curses all who practice it and fail to do it perfectly. (Galatians 3:10)

The law has nothing to do with faith. (Galatians 3:11-12)

The law was a curse that Christ redeemed us from. (Galatians 3:13)

If the law worked, God would have used it to save us. (Galatians 3:21)

Christ has abolished the law which was a wall of hostility (Ephesians 2:15)

The law is weak, useless, and makes nothing perfect. (Hebrews 7:18-19)

It is only a shadow of good things to come and will never make someone perfect. (Hebrews 10:1)

Acknowledgments

I would like to acknowledge the authors and teachers who have had a major impact on my thinking regarding the topics in this book.

Their writings are recommended in the next pages.

OTHER BOOKS & RESOURCES

Audio: Eschatology USB by Martin Trench (martintrench.com).
Video: The Star of Bethlehem DVD (bethlehemstar.net)
Video: The Great Year (binaryresearchinstitute.com)

Books

Victorious Eschatology by Harold Eberle and Martin Trench
Raptureless by Jonathan Welton
Days of Vengeance by David Chilton (a commentary on Revelation)
An Eschatology of Victory by J. Marcellus Kik
Before Jerusalem Fell by Dr. Kenneth Gentry
The Bible's Hidden Cosmology by Gordon Strachan
Jesus the Master Builder by Gordon Strachan
The Real Meaning of the Zodiac by Dr. James Kennedy
The Gospel in the Stars by Joseph A Seiss (1884)
The Witness of the Stars by E. W. Bullinger (1893)
Story in the Stars by Joe Amaral
Let There Be Light: The Seven Keys by Rocco Errico
Aramaic Light series of commentaries by George Lamsa and Rocco Errico
Aion and Aionious by John Wesley Hansen
Analytical Study of Words by Louis Abbot
Young's Literal Translation of the Bible
What the New Age is Still Saying to the Church by Dr. John Drane
The Lost World of Genesis 1 by John H Walton
Noah's Flood, Joshua's Long Day, & Lucifer's Fall by Ralph Woodrow

SELF-PUBLISHING SCHOOL

NOW IT'S YOUR TURN

Discover the EXACT 3-step blueprint you need to become a bestselling author in 3 months.

Self-Publishing School helped me, and now I want them to help you with this FREE WEBINAR!

Even if you're busy, bad at writing, or don't know where to start, you CAN write a bestseller and build your best life.

With tools and experience across a variety niches and professions, Self-Publishing School is the <u>only</u> resource you need to take your book to the finish line!

DON'T WAIT

Watch this FREE WEBINAR now, and
Say "YES" to becoming a bestseller:

www.martintrench.com/self-publishing-school

Made in the USA
Middletown, DE
12 July 2020